SEASON FOUR *Growing Out:* From Disciples To Disciplers

GROWING OTHERS

Carl Simmons

Group
Loveland, Colorado
group.com

Group resources actually work!

This Group resource incorporates our R.E.A.L. approach to ministry. It reinforces a growing friendship with Jesus, encourages long-term learning, and results in life transformation, because it's

Relational
Learner-to-learner interaction enhances learning and builds Christian friendships.

Experiential
What learners experience through discussion and action sticks with them up to 9 times longer than what they simply hear or read.

Applicable
The aim of Christian education is to equip learners to be both hearers and doers of God's Word.

Learner-based
Learners understand and retain more when the learning process takes into consideration how they learn best.

SEASON FOUR

Growing Out: From Disciples To Disciplers

GROWING OTHERS

Visit our website: **group.com**

Credits
Editor: Lee Sparks
Executive Editor: Rebecca L. Manni
Chief Creative Officer: Joani Schultz
Copy Editor: Nancy Friscia
Art Director: Paul Povolni
Book Designer: Jean Bruns
Cover Designer: Holly Voget
Illustrator: Wes Comer
Print Production: Paragon Prepress
Production Manager: Peggy Naylor

ISBN 978-0-7644-3930-8

10 9 8 7 6 5 4 3 2 1 19 18 17 16 15 14 13 12 11 10

Printed in the United States of America.

Contents

What *Growing Out* Looks Like

Growing Out is more than a series of Bible studies—it's a progression that will take you and your group from becoming disciples of Jesus to becoming discipl*ers* of *others* in Jesus. As you move through each season, you'll grow from the inside out—and as you grow, your life in Jesus will naturally expand and branch out to others in your world.

And here's the best part: As you grow out together, you'll realize how much you're *already* discipling others—starting with those in your group!

Growing Out is designed to allow you to jump in at the most appropriate place for you and your group. To help you discover your entry point, take a look at these descriptions of each season:

Season 1: Growing in Jesus focuses on developing your relationship with Jesus. Because, let's face it, the first person you have to disciple is *yourself.* More to the point, you need to learn how to let Jesus *show* you how to be his disciple. So in this season, we focus on your relationship with Jesus and how to deepen it through spiritual disciplines such as prayer, worship, Bible study…and, not least of all, through your relationships with other Christians (such as the ones you're sitting with).

After you've been grounded in your relationship with Jesus, how does that shine into the rest of your life? That's where *Season 2: Growing in Character* comes in. This season focuses on how you can invite Jesus into your most important relationships—with your family, your friends, and the people you work with—and how to keep Jesus at the center of all of them.

Season 3: Growing in Your Gifts focuses on discovering the gifts, talents, and passions God has given you and how God might want to use them to serve others—whether that's inside or outside your church walls. After this season, you'll have a better sense of who God has created you to be, and why.

And with that, you're ready for *Season 4: Growing Others.* If you've gotten this far, you've developed and deepened your walk with Jesus, you've learned how to actually live it out among those people you most care about, and you've begun to discover how God has uniquely built you. Now...how do you take what God has shown you and help *others* walk through the same process?

If you've completed Seasons 1 through 3, you already know the answer because that's *exactly* what you've been doing with your group. Season 4 will help you reach out to even more people. Call it mentoring, discipling, or just being a good Christian friend to someone who needs it, after Season 4 you'll be ready to come alongside anyone who's ready to have a deeper relationship with Jesus. Just as you were in Season 1.

In the final two seasons, you'll explore what it takes to lead others where God wants you *and* them to go next. Because as you've walked through the first four seasons, guess what? You've been growing. Others know it. And God is honoring it. So whether you see yourself that way or not, God has matured you to the point where you're ready to lead. And we're going to help you get *more* ready.

Season 5: Growing in Leadership focuses on how to stay functional even as you learn how to lead. You'll walk together through the challenges of leadership—communication, conflict resolution, building consensus, learning how to adjust your ministry, and learning to stay focused on God instead of "*your* ministry."

And as you keep growing out, God may well put things on your heart that you'll need to be the one to initiate. That brings us, at last, to *Season 6: Growing in Your Mission.* God has given you a specific vision for ministry, and now you literally need to make the dream real. We'll help walk you through the issues that come with a God-given vision. Things like, first of all, how do you know it really *is* God and not just you? How do you get others on board (and praying—a *lot*)? And how will *you* keep growing, even as the vision continues to grow and take shape?

Because, no matter where you are, you never stop *Growing Out.* God will always see to that.

Enjoy *Growing Out,* and may God bless you as you grow out together!

Why R.E.A.L. Discipleship Works

Before we go any further, go back and take one more look at the copyright page of this book (it's page 2—the one with all the credits). Go to the top of the page where it declares, "Group resources actually work!" Take a minute or two to read that entire section describing Group's R.E.A.L. guarantee, and then come back to this introduction. I'll wait for you here…

Now that we're literally back on the same page, let's explore R.E.A.L. a little more deeply. Your desire to go deeper is the reason you're reading this book, and it's not only our goal but also our *passion* to help you accomplish that desire. When it comes right down to it, there's nothing more R.E.A.L. than discipleship. Think about it:

Relational

At the heart of it, discipleship *is* relationship. First and foremost, it's about developing the most important relationship you'll ever have—your relationship with Jesus. And as your relationship with Jesus grows, it becomes far more than anything you've ever imagined.

Like any great relationship, it doesn't develop on its own. It's intentional. It's work. But it's way more than that. What we get back is far more than what we put in. How could it *not* be? It's a relationship with *Jesus.* And as that relationship grows, we'll want to bring Jesus into every other relationship we have.

So we've kept that in mind as we've designed these sessions. You'll gain a deeper understanding of God's Word, but even more important, you'll discover how to share what you've learned with those around you. And that discovery *has* to happen in community. We've made these sessions very relational because, after all, you're learning how to become discipl*ers*. By definition, that means learning how to speak God into others' lives. As you do that, you'll get as much back as you give, if not more. Because that's what happens in great relationships.

You'll notice that we often suggest getting into pairs or smaller groups. That's because participation—and learning, not to mention life change—increases when everyone's involved. It's more challenging, sure, but it's also more rewarding. Be sure to take advantage of the times we suggest it.

All this is a long way of saying that by the time you've finished this season, you'll not only have a deeper relationship with Jesus, but your spiritual relationships with others will be richer and deeper than you had ever anticipated. And when that happens, be sure to thank us; a little affirmation goes a long way toward helping us to keep doing what we do here.

Experiential

Experiences? Yeah, we've got experiences. And as you discover together where God wants to take you next, you'll have experiences of your own long after you've completed these sessions.

Research has proven again and again that the more senses we engage in the learning process, the more likely a session is to stick and truly become woven into our daily lives. Jesus knew that, too. That's why he used everyday items to make his message more real. Not only that, but he invited people out of their comfort zones to conquer their fear of the unknown. We like to do that, too. A lot.

And because it's so different from what we're used to when studying God's Word, this is often the hardest part of R.E.A.L. learning for people to embrace. Is it *really* OK to have fun when we're studying the Bible? Does it truly honor God? Wouldn't it distract us from focusing on God?

First, let's make it clear that these are legitimate concerns. I've wrestled with all of them as I've developed these sessions. We want to honor Jesus. Discipleship isn't a joke. It's serious business. It's about the rest of your life and how you'll glorify God with it. There's nothing more serious than that.

Nonetheless, sometimes the best way to get serious is to set aside our expectations first, so we're able to open up and get down to what we're *really* wrestling with, rather than just come up with the right answers, go home, and never really deal with the things God wants us to deal with. The experiences in this book go a long way toward accomplishing that. Here are just a few of the ways people "got R.E.A.L." as we field-tested this curriculum:

- A church elder in our group declared from the beginning, in no uncertain terms and with a bit of a growl, "I don't *do* games." A few weeks in, he shared, "This is exactly what [my wife and I] needed right now." Several weeks later, this same game-hating elder proclaimed, "I really *liked* that activity! It worked *perfectly!*"
- One of our hosts, who also prepared the session's snack, suggested, "I'll make sure I pull it out of the oven just when everyone gets here." She understood that not only the look and taste of the snack but also the smell would help people experience the session more acutely.
- A pastor in our group enjoyed one particular activity so much that he went ahead and used it in his own church's small-group training class.
- Another woman shared how her husband had been initially skeptical about R.E.A.L. learning and about small groups in general. (Anyone else detecting a pattern among the men, by the way?) Several sessions later, she was positively glowing as she shared how we'd "broken through" and how much he'd opened up as we'd gone along—and for that matter, how he was still talking about the session the next morning.

Discipleship *is* a lifelong adventure. And we're here to help you embrace that adventure. Together. That's why we've not only built in activities to get you thinking about your faith (and expressing it) in brand-new ways, but...well, let's just move on to...

Applicable

This is pretty straightforward. You're here not only to learn but also to grow. And that means taking what you've learned and using it.

We give you opportunities in every session to do that—to give you a safe place to experiment, if you will. We also provide opportunities at the end of each session for you to take what you've learned and "Walk It Out" in the rest of your life—so that your faith *becomes* your life, and you can take practical steps toward sharing your life in Jesus so others can see and respond to it as well.

Learner-Based

For some of you, the Bible passages and ideas you're studying may be familiar. But as you explore them in fresh ways in these sessions, you'll experience and understand God's Word in ways you've never considered before. We're studying God's living Word, after all. So we want to help you not only learn brand-new things but also find new significance and meaning in familiar and taken-for-granted ideas.

Therefore, we've been very deliberate about choosing the right approaches for the right sessions. When an activity works, let's get up and do it. If a movie clip brings out the meaning of what you're learning, throw in the DVD and let's talk. If a snack not only works as an icebreaker but also as a discussion starter about a much deeper subject, let's serve it up and dig in. And when it's time to just open up God's Word and really wrap our minds around what God wants us to understand about a given subject—or to be reminded of what God has already shown us (because we forget that all too easily, too)—then we'll bust out our Bibles and read as many passages as it takes to begin to grasp (or re-grasp) that.

You're also here to discover who *you* are in Jesus. The body of Christ is made of millions of unique parts. You're one of them. We *know* one size doesn't fit all, and we've built *Growing Out* to reflect that. So whatever reaches you best—the Bible study, the activities, the questions, the take-home pieces, whatever—use them to their fullest extent. I'll give you some more ideas of how to do this in the next two sections.

However you approach these sessions—and whether you do that as a leader or as a participant—be sure to help others in your group approach things in the ways God can best reach them. And as God works in all of you, celebrate it. A lot.

May God bless you as you begin your journey together. And as God takes each of you to the places and experiences he has prepared for you, never forget: You're all in this together. You, God, and everyone he puts in your path. And *that's* discipleship.

—Carl Simmons

About the Sessions

Now that you know why we do what we do, let's talk about *how* we do it—and more important—how *you* can do it.

You may already understand this, but just so we're clear: Discipleship is *not* about completing a curriculum. It's about developing and deepening the most important spiritual relationships you have—first with God, then with those God brings you in contact with—because *none* of those relationships is an accident. They're all intentional, and we need to be intentional as well.

In fact, that's why we refer to each study as a season, rather than as a study, book, or quarter. Each of us grows at our own pace. Your season of growth might be longer or shorter than someone else's, and that's OK. God will take as long as you need to get you where he wants you. So spend as much time in each season as you need to. But stay committed to moving forward.

Also, each season has been built so that whether you're a participant or a leader, you can get the most out of each session. And that starts with the layout of each lesson. Keep a finger here, flip over to one of the sessions, and let's look at why this is so different.

This isn't just a leader guide. It's not just a guide for group members. It's *both*! And the way we've set up the sessions reflects that.

Leaders: The left-hand pages contain *your* instructions, so you're constantly on track and know what's happening next. What you do, what you say—all the basics are there. You'll also want to be sure to check out the "Leader Notes" beginning on page 165—they'll give you specific prep instructions for each session as well as great tips to make each session the best it can be.

Group Members: You don't care about all that leader stuff, do you? Didn't think so. Now you don't need to. The right-hand pages are just for you. Write your answers, journal whatever else God is saying to you, record insights from your group discussions, doodle while you listen—you've got plenty of room for all of it. All the questions and Bible passages you'll be using are right there. Use your pages to get the most out of what God's showing you each week.

Got all that? Good. Now let's talk about what each session looks like.

Come and See In this (usually) brief opening section, you'll take time to unwind and transition from wherever you're coming from—a hectic drive to church on a Sunday morning or the end of a busy day—into the theme of the session. You and your group might enjoy a snack or a movie clip together; maybe it'll be an activity; maybe you'll just talk with someone else. Then you'll be ready to dig in deep. And maybe—because you were too busy having such a good time doing it—you won't even realize that you've already gotten down to business.

Seek and Find This is the heart of each session, and it's usually the longest section. You'll spend roughly a half-hour digging into God's Word and discovering its meaning in a way you hadn't realized before. You think you understand these things now? Just *wait.* Through a variety of experiences and powerful questions that take a fresh look both at Scripture and at what's going on in your own head and heart, you'll discover how God's Word *really* applies to your life.

Go Now you'll move from understanding how what you've been studying applies to your life, to considering ways to act on it. Again, through meaningful experiences and questions, you'll discover what you can do with what God has shown you through today's session. Which will take you directly into…

Walk It Out This is the take-home part of the session. With a partner or partners, you'll each choose a weekly challenge to apply this session to your life in practical ways in the coming week and beyond.

We've broken out the challenges very specifically, to meet you wherever you are. And because of the nature of this season—*Growing Others*—the challenges are broken out a little differently than they were in earlier seasons. This season, the challenge you take on *will* involve someone else. Therefore, you'll get the options to "Walk It Out"…

☐ …as it comes

Some of you may not have in mind a specific person you want to invest in, at least at first. So this first option offers some easy, on-the-spot ideas to walk out what you've learned with others you may have just met.

☐ …with my family

The first people you need to help grow (after yourself) are those in your family. You'll get ideas on how to do that here.

☐ …with my friends

This option might be the obvious choice for many of you. You know who you want to invest in and draw closer to Jesus with. But what's your next step? If you don't already know, try *this* one.

☐ …with my group

This might be an outreach event, a retreat, or just a special get-together outside your session time. Every so often, try one of these ideas as a group, and see what God does with it.

By the way, if God has really spoken to you about something else during a session and you know you need to do whatever he's urging you to do, don't feel you have to choose from the ideas we've provided. Be obedient. Share what God is showing you with your group so they can pray for you and encourage you.

There's one more section to tell you about. It appears at the very end. It's not even part of the session per se, but it could end up meaning a lot to you.

Go Deeper I can't emphasize this enough, so I'm repeating it: Discipleship is *not* about completing a curriculum. It's about developing and deepening the most important spiritual relationships you have—first with God, then with those God has brought you in contact with—because *none* of those relationships is an accident.

Therefore, it's possible you'll work through this season and think, Before I go any further, I *really* need a deeper understanding of... That's why I've provided a list of resources at the end of each session to help you dig deeper. At Group, we're not shy about recommending other publishers—and if a resource applies to more than one area of spiritual growth, we'll recommend it more than once. This isn't about selling Group products (although there's always much more dancing in the halls here when that happens). It's about your growing relationship with Jesus and your willingness to invite God into whatever you're still wrestling with.

And that painful thing you're feeling when you do that? That's called growth. But the good news is: We're in this together. So pull over whenever you need to! Or jump right into the next season. We're here for you either way.

Which brings us to a little reminder: If there's an area in which you'd like to see *us* dig deeper and create more resources to help *you*, tell us! Write to us at Group Publishing, Inc., P.O. Box 481, Loveland, CO 80539; or contact us via e-mail at smallgroupministry.com. We'd love to hear what you're thinking. (Yes—*really*!)

Choose Your Environment

Growing Out works well in a variety of venues. We want to help you wherever you are. Don't be shy about trying any of them! Here are some additional ideas, depending on your venue.

Sunday School

First, you may have noticed that I've chosen the word *group* instead of *class* throughout. Not every group is a class, but every class is a group. You're not here just to study and learn facts—you're also here to learn how to live out what you've learned. Together. As a group. We hope that becomes even truer as you work through these sessions.

We've constructed these sessions to run an hour at a brisk pace, but we understand the limitations a Sunday school program can put on the amount of time you spend on a session. So if a great question has started a great discussion and you don't want to cut it off, feel free to trim back elsewhere as needed. For example, since much of our field test group was made up of couples who could talk on the way home, we discovered that making Walk It Out a take-home instead of an in-class piece was one good way to buy back time without losing impact.

Try not to be one of those groups that say, "Great—we can skip that experience now!" Remember, the more senses and learning styles you engage, the more these sessions will stick. So play with these activities. Give yourself permission to fail—but go in expecting God to do the unexpected.

And if you don't have specific time limitations, read on.

Small Groups

If you need more than an hour for a session—and you're not tied to a clock or a calendar—take it! Again, taking the time to understand what God wants to tell your group is *way* more important than covering the material or staying within the one-hour or 13-week parameters. This happened repeatedly while in our field test. When the session inspired great discussion and people got down to things they were really wrestling with, we decided we'd explore the session further the following week.

Learn to recognize rabbit trails—and get off them sooner rather than later—but don't short-circuit those occasions when the Holy Spirit is really working in people's lives. Those occasions will happen often in these sessions. If you're having a rich discussion and are really digging in, take an extra week and dig even deeper. Give the full meaning of the session time to sink in.

One-on-One Discipleship

Although this curriculum is designed for a larger group setting, we absolutely don't want to discourage you from using it in a more traditional, one-on-one discipleship setting. True, some of the activities might not work in a setting this small, and if that's the case, feel free to bypass them and go directly into the Bible passages and questions—there are plenty left to work with. The important thing is that you work together through the issues and at the pace that works for you.

But don't take this as an opportunity to entirely excuse yourselves from experiences—have a little fun together, and see what God does. Allow yourselves to be surprised.

Also—and it's probably obvious for this and the next scenario—all those recommendations we make to form smaller groups or twosomes? You can skip those and jump right into the discussion or activity.

Smaller Groups or Accountability Groups

One more thing: We don't want to discourage you from doing one-on-one discipleship, especially if you've already got a good thing going. There are some great and healthy mentoring relationships out there, and if you're already involved in one, keep at it! That said, research has shown repeatedly that learning can happen at a more accelerated rate—and more profoundly—in settings other than the traditional teacher-student relationship. So if you're just starting out, consider gathering in groups of three or four.

- It's an environment that allows everyone to learn from one another. While there's often still a clear leader, the playing field feels more level, and the conversations often become more open and honest.
- If one person leaves for any reason—and there are plenty of legitimate ones—the group or accountability relationship isn't finished. Everyone else presses forward. No one is left hanging.
- The dynamics of a group of three or four are simpler than those of larger groups. And a group of three or four can be the best of both worlds, offering the rich discussions of a large group and the intimacy and accountability of one-on-one relationships.
- Again, we're about creating discipl*ers*, and a smaller group allows growing disciplers to test-drive their own instructions, struggles, and transparency in an environment in which they can be both honestly critiqued and wholeheartedly encouraged. And when that happens, growth happens—for everyone.

If you'd like to delve into this further, Greg Ogden's *Transforming Discipleship* (InterVarsity) is a great resource to get you started, as are any number of materials from ChurchSmart Resources (churchsmart.com).

Whatever setting or environment you use for *Growing Out,* use it to its fullest. May God bless your efforts and those of the people with whom you share life!

Getting Connected

Pass your books around the room, and have people write their names, phone numbers, e-mail addresses, and birthdays in the spaces provided. Then make it a point to stay in touch during the week.

name	phone	e-mail	birthday

So You Want to Grow a Christian...

"*Jesus came and told his disciples, 'I have been given all authority in heaven and on earth. Therefore, go and make disciples of all the nations, baptizing them in the name of the Father and the Son and the Holy Spirit. Teach these new disciples to obey all the commands I have given you. And be sure of this: I am with you always, even to the end of the age'* " (MATTHEW 28:18-20).

In this session, we'll journey...

from → **to**

realizing the need to invest in others' lives and what holds us back from doing it...

identifying those people we can invest in and how to get started.

Before gathering, make sure you have...

- ○ newsprint tablet, blackboard, or white board
- ○ a pitcher of (preferably hot) water and a few tea bags*

*See **Leader Notes**, page 167, for details.

Come and See

(about 15 minutes)

Leaders: Please note that the bolded sections of text are for you to read aloud. Feel free to change the wording to make yourself more comfortable. Or just use ours; that's why it's here.

Ask people to get into gender-specific groups of three. (A group of two people is OK, if necessary. But three is preferable, and groups should not be larger than three people.) Gender-specific groups will help everyone feel free to share honestly and feel as safe as possible. Give everyone a minute for introductions, and then regain everyone's attention.

» **Since this session—really, this entire season—is about helping other Christians grow, let's start by reflecting on our own journeys so far. Think about a time you experienced a huge growth spurt in your life. If you can't think of a spiritual example off the bat, share an example from your professional or personal life.**

(Pause for about 10 seconds.)

» **Got an example in your heads? Good. Now in your groups, briefly talk about that time, and then discuss these questions:**

Allow 10 minutes for discussion, and then regain everyone's attention.

> *Reflect on your own life. Isn't it true that change has not come only through the formal ministry of the Word? Hasn't God also used ordinary people to change your heart and transform your life?*
>
> *—Paul David Tripp,* Instruments in the Redeemer's Hands

» **You just shared about an important time in your life and about the people who helped and maybe even inspired you. It probably felt good just to think about those people again. But as good as those people made us feel, it's even more rewarding to *be* that kind of person—to know that God has truly used us to help others.**

Any work we do that has eternal value involves other people—whether it involves serving them, praying for them, being a good parent, or simply being a good friend. Everything we do can potentially have an eternal impact on others. Think about it: How others have loved you—or failed to—is part of the reason you are who you are today.

◎ When did you first realize that you had somehow taken a giant leap forward? What was different?

◎ Who helped you most in taking that leap? What did he or she (or they) do to keep you moving forward?

We'll be spending this season learning more about what God expects us to spend a lifetime learning and doing—making and growing disciples of Jesus. We're going to learn how to help others move forward—and how God moves *us* forward when we trust and follow him. The group you're with right now is going to help you. For this entire season, the people you're sitting with now will be your subgroup. So get to know them because you'll be working together for a while. Learn to love them. And move forward together with them.

So let's start right now. Stay seated in your groups, and let's begin to dig in together.

Seek and Find

(about 30 minutes)

Ask for a volunteer to read Matthew 28:16-20, and then discuss:

Nondiscipleship is the elephant in the church…The fundamental negative reality among Christian believers now is their failure to be constantly learning how to live their lives in The Kingdom Among Us. And it is an accepted reality.

—Dallas Willard, The Divine Conspiracy

Write down everyone's responses on your white board. Once you've got a sizeable list, continue your discussion.

» **When we think of discipling others, it's also easy to get caught up in thinking, I can't do this (for whatever reason), I need to learn more first, I need to accomplish more first, or I need to have more credibility with that person before I open my mouth. And these might well be issues we need to work on. But very often these issues become excuses or unnecessary roadblocks we set up for ourselves. Most of the time, it's only fear of the unknown that holds us back. We make it about what we think *we* can do rather than what Jesus *commands* us to do and what *he* promises to do as we step out in faith.**

Matthew 28:16-20

◎ What comes to mind when you hear the phrase *make disciples*? List as many things as you can.

◎ Let's stop and look at our list. What thoughts or emotions are you having right now as you look it over?

◎ Look at our passage again. What does Jesus tell us about himself?

◎ How would believing and better understanding what Jesus tells us about himself help us keep our list in perspective? How would it change the way we do some of these things? Be specific.

Seek and Find continued

The first and maybe the biggest step to becoming an effective discipler is simply to show up—and make the most of the situation God has called you into. Hasn't God brought you through a lot already? More than anything, *that's* what God wants to show others through you. Not your perfect answers or your unbelievable heart, but what *God has done*—and, therefore, what God can do for that other person, too.

Discuss these questions together in your groups: ⟶

"I gain more of Christ in one converted sinner and growing saint than in a hundred ordinary chores."

—John Piper, Desiring God

◎ Who do you know who seems ready to take the next step spiritually—whether he or she's already growing as a Christian, a brand-new Christian, or a not-yet Christian?

◎ If you could help that person understand just one thing right now, what would it be?

◎ If you've already shared that one thing with him or her, what do you think that person needs to really get it? If you haven't shared it yet, what's holding you back?

◎ Now consider *this*: How could spending more time with that person help *you* grow closer to Jesus?

Go

(about 20 minutes)

Bring out your pitcher of water, and drop your tea bags in it, if you haven't already.

» **Think again about the people you just discussed. For this season, we want you to make two commitments—one to the group you're with and one to that person or persons God has put on your heart, even if those people don't know it yet!**

Think of our group here as your laboratory—a safe place where you can experiment, play with ideas, and see what works and what doesn't. We're not all built the same, and a great idea for one person might feel totally fake for another. That's OK. Play with ideas during your time here to discover what God *does* want you to use.

Then commit to the people you've already thought of. Try to seek them out this week, and ask them to commit to a regular time with you. Remember, you don't have to be the expert or teacher here. You're just a fellow traveler headed toward Jesus, one who wants to work through things with another traveler.

Some people might hear the words *accountability* or *discipleship* and say, "I'm in. When do we get started?" It's more likely, though, that many will be intimidated by that kind of talk. So don't bash people over the head with this. Invite them out to lunch or a cup of coffee for starters. Talk about *their* lives and the things that are most on *their* minds and hearts right now. Then ask whether they might want to make a regular time out of it. Most people will accept your offer if they know you're serious about committing to them and don't feel overwhelmed by the commitment. A weekly time together is best, but if schedules only allow for biweekly or monthly, that's OK. Start there and see where things go.

You can even say something like, "I'm taking a class on

> *What would happen if we were to focus on the four out of every ten adults and one out of every three teenagers who have already asked Jesus Christ to be their Savior—and do everything we can to help them grow into inspired, unmistakable disciples of Jesus?*
>
> —George Barna, Growing True Disciples

discipleship, and I'd like to try out some of the things I'm learning on a real person. *You're* a real person—would you mind helping me work through this?" Once the person is done laughing, he or she will probably say yes.

Can we commit to that?

Wait for responses.

» Now let's look at our pitcher that's been sitting here and what's been happening while we've been talking.

▼ GROUP

◎ What things had to take place for our tea bags to change the water?

◎ So what normally holds you back from "getting into the water"—and staying there—with others?

◎ What's the first step you can take to overcome that?

Get back into your groups, and move on together to the section called Walk It Out. Let's plan to come back together in five minutes.

LEADER ▼

Walk It Out

(about 5 minutes)

» The following options are here to help you put what you've learned into practice. But if God has prompted you to do something else through this session, then by all means do that!

GROUP ▼

I'll walk it out...

choose 1:

☐ ...as it comes

Identify one person you know casually who's not a Christian. Instead of making that person a "project," become that person's friend. Pray for him or her regularly, and wait for the natural opportunities that God brings to talk about spiritual things. Take the first step toward building a friendship with that person before this group meets again.

☐ ...with my family

Who in your family has been receiving less time and attention than he or she needs? Start making up for that this week. Set aside time to get together and get caught up. Be sure to make it about the other person rather than about you. Ask about his or her needs, and simply listen.

☐ ...with my friends

If you have a significant relationship where something's missing (especially if that something is Jesus), take a risk. Tell that person about this study, and humbly ask what it would take for you to have a more positive impact on his or her life. Avoid the temptation to defend yourself or ask anything in return. Rather, commit to making a difference in the way you interact.

Form pairs, select the option you'd like to take on this week, and share your choice with your partner. Write what you plan to do in the space provided, and make plans to connect with your partner before the next session to check in and encourage each other. Take five minutes to do that now.

☐ **...with my group** This week's assignment is simple: Set aside a block of time to get to know each other. Although an hour a week for the next few months will certainly build your relationships, don't depend entirely on the time you'll have together here. Hang out informally. Get together for coffee. Do some kind of activity together. What do you all like? What's something you'd like to try together? Share some experiences *outside* this setting.

...or think of your own!

Because God wants me to get into the water, I'll "Walk It Out" by:

Walk It Out continued

prayer ➔

Come back together as a large group. Thank God for all he's done in your life, and ask God to help each of you "go and make disciples." Ask God to help you see the value in the people placed in your journey, and to see that those people are far more important than the things that discourage us from reaching out to them. Confess to God your unwillingness to change—and then ask God to change you anyway, so he can use you to change the lives of those around you.

And then, if you like, enjoy some tea together!

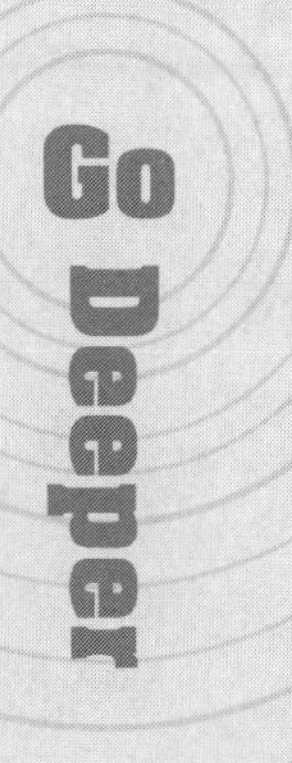

To dig deeper into how to invest in the lives of others—Christian and not-yet Christian alike—here are some great resources:

Sacred Companions: The Gift of Spiritual Friendship and Direction by David G. Benner (InterVarsity)

Spiritual Fathers: Restoring the Reproductive Church by Dan Schaffer (Building Brothers)

Spiritual Friend: Reclaiming the Gift of Spiritual Direction by Tilden Edwards (Paulist)

The Mentor Handbook: Detailed Guidelines and Helps for Christian Mentors and Mentorees by J. Robert Clinton and Richard W. Clinton (Barnabas)

Spiritual Mentoring: A Guide for Seeking and Giving Direction by Keith R. Anderson and Randy D. Reese (InterVarsity)

Is this an area where you'd like to see *us* dig deeper and create more resources? Do you have a great idea we ought to consider? Let us know at info@group.com. We'd love to hear what you're thinking.

The Meaning of Commitment

"As apostles of Christ we certainly had a right to make some demands of you, but instead we were like children among you. Or we were like a mother feeding and caring for her own children. We loved you so much that we shared with you not only God's Good News but our own lives, too" (1 THESSALONIANS 2:7-8).

In this session, we'll journey...

from seeing the importance of committing long-term to others... → **to** determining how we can make those commitments happen.

Before gathering, make sure you have...

Optional activities (choose one or both):

Come and See

- ○ **Option A:** Your greeting time in Come and See
- ○ **Option B:** DVD of *Dances With Wolves* (see page 43)

Go

- ○ **Option A:** Discussion of 1 Thessalonians 2
- ○ **Option B:** DVD Another scene from *Dances With Wolves* (see page 44)

See **Leader Notes**, page 168, for details.

Come and See

(about 15 minutes)

If you've chosen **Option A**, *read on.*
If you're doing **Option B**, *go to page 43.*

Ask people to get into their groups from last week.

» **This week you're going to spend a little more time introducing yourselves to one another—but you're going to do it a little differently. Find someone in another group, and take 30 seconds to share with each other one outstanding example of commitment you know about. Go!**

Allow a minute for pairs to greet and share.

» **Find someone in another group, and take another 30 seconds each to share about a formal commitment you've made—to a job or a team, for example—and how that commitment changed over time.**

If you have a small group with only a couple of subgroups, encourage people to get with another person in the other group. Again, allow only a minute for pairs to share.

» **Find one more person, and share about the longest commitment you've made to another person—such as a marriage or a friendship. This time take a minute each to share how that commitment has changed *you* over time.**

After two more minutes, have everyone sit down. Discuss these questions:

» **Getting to know new people can be exciting for some—and terrifying for others. God *can* use a chance encounter to do something meaningful, but the most meaningful encounters most of us will ever have will**

◎ What was enjoyable about this activity? What wasn't so enjoyable?

◎ How was this "meet-and-greet" like some of the relationships you have right now?

◎ What do you do to get past that meet-and-greet stage and actually get to know someone?

be with the people we stick with over the long haul. Because we experience each other's highs and lows together, we and our friends are changed.

Now put Jesus in the center of those relationships. When that happens, our relationships take on a character greater than anything we could ever have imagined. And it's something we'll want to see happen in every relationship we have. So let's explore how our commitment to Jesus and our commitment to others can come together to become something extraordinary—something that truly glorifies God.

Seek and Find

(about 25 minutes)

» Let's look at several passages of Scripture that show us what a deep, committed friendship looks like. Read the passage(s) your group is assigned, and briefly discuss the particular nature of the friendship described in that passage. Then apply the two questions to your passage. We'll come back together in 15 minutes.

Divide the following sets of passages among groups:

- Ruth 1:3-18
- 1 Samuel 20:1-17 and 24-34
- 1 Kings 19:19-21 and 2 Kings 2:1-14
- Acts 9:21-28 and 11:19-26
- 1 Timothy 4:11-16 and 2 Timothy 1:3-10

Allow 15 minutes, and then come back together. Ask groups to briefly summarize their passages and their answers, and then discuss these questions together:

"[Y]ou should enter with trepidation into the deep and genuine concern for those few persons God has committed to your care—your family, your students, your employees, your parishioners. This concern is an involvement, a distraction, and it is vitally urgent."

—Thomas Merton, Conjectures of a Guilty Bystander

Ruth 1:3-18; 1 Samuel 20:1-17 and 24-34; 1 Kings 19:19-21 and 2 Kings 2:1-14; Acts 9:21-28 and 11:19-26; 1 Timothy 4:11-16 and 2 Timothy 1:3-10

◎ What are some legitimate—or at least common—reasons the friends in your passages could have used to back out of their commitments?

◎ What kept them going anyway?

◎ Which do you enjoy more—being committed to a lot of people you can help in smaller bursts, or having a deeper commitment to just a few people? Why?

◎ How could working together with someone who answered differently make a huge difference in someone else's life? What could each of you bring that the other can't?

Go

(about 20 minutes)

If you've chosen **Option A**, *read on.*
If you're doing **Option B**, *go to page 44.*

» **This season we're focused on how God can use us to grow others—and on the way God has built each of us to do that. Think about those relationships you want to take to the next level. You probably have at least one in mind already. You don't need to name names here, but keep those people in mind as we read both 1 Thessalonians 2:7-13 and the Dietrich Bonhoeffer quote on page 39.**

Ask for volunteers to read 1 Thessalonians 2:7-13 and the Dietrich Bonhoeffer quote, and then discuss the following questions: →

» **We're going to spend a lot more time exploring the answers to that last question in our next session. But for now, keep thinking about your answers. We need each other in order to grow. Having friends who can help us is a huge factor in making that happen.**

So let's proceed to Walk It Out.

> *The Christian, however, must bear the burden of a brother. He must suffer and endure the brother. It is only when he is a burden that another person is really a brother and not merely an object to be manipulated.*
>
> *—Dietrich Bonhoeffer,*
> Life Together

1 Thessalonians 2:7-13

◎ What keeps you from "suffer[ing] and endur[ing]" some of the people God puts in your life?

◎ What would need to change in you for you to feel prepared to take on that person's burden—and become a better friend to him or her?

◎ Who could help you make those changes? What would you ask that person to do? Be specific.

LEADER ▼

Walk It Out

(about 5 minutes)

» **The following options are here to help you put what you've learned into practice. But if God has prompted you to do something else through this session, then by all means do that!**

GROUP ▼

I'll walk it out...

choose 1:

☐ ...as it comes

Encourage one person this week whom you don't know well. When you see the opportunity, go to that person and share something specific that would be a real encouragement to him or her. Then see where that goes. As further opportunities to talk to or pray for that person arise, use them.

☐ ...with my family

Who in your family could use encouragement right now? Make time for your spouse or child this week. But don't just do it as a one-time thing. Use this week's time together as a starting point, and keep following up with him or her. Keep talking. Pray together. God will do amazing things with your time, and it may well become your favorite time of the week.

☐ ...with my friends

Do something out-of-the-box with your friend this week. Think of an activity you'd both enjoy doing but for some reason haven't done together. Then make a plan to go do it. Doing serious stuff together isn't the only way to build a friendship. Build memories. Have fun!

Form pairs, select the option you'd like to take on this week, and share your choice with your partner. Write what you plan to do in the space provided, and make plans to connect with your partner before the next session to check in and encourage each other. Take five minutes to do that now.

Walk It Out

☐ **...with my group** What group of people might your group consider committing to? Think of a service project your group could do—*outside* your church—and then make it happen. Set aside time afterward to discuss how working together as a group both helped others and drew you closer together. Consider ways you could make this a regular occurrence.

...or think of your own!

Because God wants me to commit to others the way God has committed to me, I'll "Walk It Out" by:

___

___

___

___

___

___

___

Walk It Out continued

prayer

Come back together as a group. Pray about the commitments you just made during Walk It Out, pray for those people you intend to make deeper and longer-lasting commitments to, and pray for the steps God wants you to take next. Ask God to open your eyes to the possibilities as your relationships go deeper.

For those wanting to camp out and dig deeper into how to how to make a lasting commitment in others' lives, here are some great resources:

Dare to Be Uncommon: Discovering How to Impact Your World by Tony Dungy (Group)

Every Man's a Mentor by Sam Mehaffie (Xulon)

Eternal Impact: Investing in the Lives of Others by Phil Downer with Chip MacGregor (Eternal Impact)

Becoming a Woman of Influence: Making a Lasting Impact on Others by Carol Kent (NavPress)

SEEING IT DIFFERENTLY

Come and See–Option B

LEADER Instead of your meet-and-greet time, watch a scene from the movie *Dances With Wolves*. Cue the movie to 48:00 (DVD Chapter 7), as John Dunbar runs after the Sioux stealing his horses.

Before starting, say, **If you're not familiar with this movie, this is the first encounter between Lieutenant John Dunbar and the warrior Wind in His Hair. Take special note of Wind in His Hair's words and how he says them; it'll come in handy later in our session.**

Stop the clip at 49:32, as John passes out, and then discuss:

GROUP

◎ When have you had a first encounter with someone go wrong from the start? Talk about it a little.

◎ Were you ever able to get to know that person better, and if so, what did it take to make that happen?

Pick up at the leader statement on page 34, beginning **Getting to know new people can be exciting for some—and terrifying for others...**

SEEING IT DIFFERENTLY

Go–Option B

LEADER Instead of the discussion of 1 Thessalonians 2, watch another scene from *Dances With Wolves*. Cue the movie to 2:52:57 (DVD Chapter 24), as John Dunbar (now also Dances With Wolves) and Stands With a Fist are riding away. Stop the clip at 2:54:05, as Wind in His Hair gives one last cry.

Anyone else notice the similarities between Wind in His Hair's first words to John and the ones he uses here? (Pause.) **If you're familiar with the movie, hold on to your answers for our next question:**

GROUP

◎ If you're *not* familiar with this movie, what must have taken place for this radical change to occur in Wind in His Hair's attitude?

Once those not familiar with the movie have answered, let those familiar with the movie chime in. Then continue your discussion:

GROUP

◎ What does (or would) it feel like to have this kind of friendship? Explain.

◎ Maybe the person God is calling you to reach out to isn't an enemy, but what would have to take place for things to change from where you are to a friendship like this one?

Go on to Walk It Out on page 40.

You Can't Do It Alone

"But you know how Timothy has proved himself. Like a son with his father, he has served with me in preaching the Good News" (PHILIPPIANS 2:22).

In this session, we'll journey...

from → **to**

re-examining the different levels of relationships in your spiritual growth...

identifying others who can invest in you as you invest in others.

Before gathering, make sure you have...

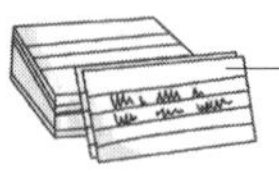

- ○ notecards or small sheets of paper for everyone
- ○ pencils or pens for everyone

See **Leader Notes**, page 169, for details.

Come and See

(about 10 minutes)

Get in your groups, and discuss:

After five minutes, come back together. Share highlights and insights from your small-group discussion.

» **Our lives are always changing, whether we realize it or not. For example, we're gathered here so we can continue to learn how to make the shift from being simply a disciple of Jesus to becoming a discipler of others. You're probably facing other transitions in life as well.**

The good news is you don't have to face those challenges alone. And you're not meant to. God has been growing us and equipping us to share our lives in Jesus with others all along. At the same time, God still wants us to seek support from others—to share our lives in Jesus with those we trust, so they can help us move forward even as we help others. We're going to focus on one specific type of relationship today, but before we do, let's take one more big picture view of the kinds of relationships every Christian needs in order to grow.

> *If I genuinely bring myself to a relationship, I must be prepared to be changed by it.*
>
> *—David G. Benner,* Sacred Companions

◎ Think about a time you made a major transition, such as a move, a new job or position, or a major change in your family. Who helped you most through those changes?

◎ How did that person help you most? Be specific.

Seek and Find

(about 25 minutes)

Ask for a volunteer to read 1 John 2:12-14. Then discuss these questions: →

» **We need all kinds of people to help us grow. More mature Christians show us how to live out the things we still struggle with. They know Jesus, and they model him to us. They show us, "You can do this." Those wrestling with similar issues of faith and life help us gain new perspective, and they help us know we've won the biggest battle of all even as we continue fighting the little battles together. Even those who are younger in their faith can teach us incredible things. They help us see God through fresh eyes. They remind us of things in our faith we need to never forget. And they remind us that how we help *them* in Jesus...matters.**

You've spent the last couple of weeks thinking of others you can invest in—whether they are people just beginning to walk with Jesus or people you can grow alongside. Today we're going to focus on relationships with more mature Christians who are willing and available to help us move forward.

Let's start by taking another look at one of the best-known examples of a more mature Christian bringing a younger one forward—Paul and Timothy. We spent a little time with them last week; let's spend a little more time this week looking at the end result. Would someone please read Philippians 2:19-24? →

> *"It is never a waste of time to remind people of who they are in Christ. Doing so stimulates hope, courage, and faith."*
>
> *—Paul David Tripp,* Instruments in the Redeemer's Hands

 **1 John 2:12-14**

◎ What stages of growth are described in this passage? What good things does John have to say about each of them?

◎ What stage do you feel you're in right now? How do John's words speak to where you are?

 **Philippians 2:19-24**

◎ Imagine being a Philippian reading or hearing this for the first time. What impressions would you have had of Timothy?

◎ Paul takes pride in being like a "father" to Timothy. Who has served as a "father" or "mother" to you, giving you faith examples that have helped you grow?

◎ How do you see that person's faith reflected in you today?

◎ How have you been able to pass on what that person taught you to others? And if you haven't, can you think of someone who could benefit from that person's wisdom?

Go

(about 25 minutes)

> *Our brother breaks the circle of self-deception. A man who confesses his sins in the presence of a brother knows that he is no longer alone with himself; he experiences the presence of God in the reality of the other person.*
>
> —*Dietrich Bonhoeffer,* Life Together

» Now I'm going to ask you to do something a bit unusual. For the next few minutes, forget everything you know about Paul and Timothy. Pretend our last two sessions haven't happened. You've never read *anything* about them. For that matter, pretend you know nothing at all about Paul except what we're about to read here.

Get back into your groups, read 1 Timothy 1:12-19, and take 10 minutes to discuss this question:

Gather people's attention after 10 minutes, keeping them in their groups.

» OK, you now have permission to remember what you know about Paul and Timothy. Even if it's something you haven't read in the last couple of weeks, it's OK to bring it into our discussion now. And with that in mind, let's discuss these questions:

Give everyone a notecard or paper and a pen.

» Think again about the questions you'd ask Paul. Whom do you know—or would like to get to know—to ask those questions? Write that person's name on your card, and rewrite your questions on that card as well.

Allow up to a minute for everyone to write.

» In your groups, share about the person whose name you wrote, why you chose him or her, and what you'd ask. Then talk about the next steps you're going to take to connect with that person.

When you're done sharing, look at the Walk It Out options together. Share your choices, and then pray for one another. Ask God to open doors between

1 Timothy 1:12-19

◎ If you were to meet Paul in person right now—based solely on what you know from this passage—what one thing would you ask him for advice about? Why?

◎ Why was Paul the right person to grow Timothy? What did he supply that Timothy lacked?

◎ How did Timothy's gifts and personality complement Paul's? How was he able to help accomplish what Paul couldn't do on his own?

each of you and the people whose names you wrote on your cards. Then ask God to show you how to take what you've learned today and "Walk It Out."

When you're done, you're free to quietly leave [or quietly hang out until everyone's finished, if you're in a small-group setting].

LEADER ▼

Walk It Out

(about 5 minutes)

» **The following options are here to help you put what you've learned into practice. But if God has prompted you to do something else through this session, then by all means do that!**

GROUP ▼

I'll walk it out...

choose 1:

☐ ...as it comes

What transitions are you now facing? Who could you sit down with over lunch or coffee to help you think them through? Make time with him or her this week. It might even be with the person you've written down on your card.

☐ ...with my family

Here's a thought: How can your family mentor you? It's true, family members may already regularly remind you about your "areas needing improvement." Then again, they know you best, right? So take their input seriously, and actually ask for it this week. Invite them to be honest with you and to tell you how you could be more Christ-like with them. Then think of ways you can immediately apply their suggestions.

☐ ...with my friends

This one probably requires a bit of humility, but ask yourself which of your friends could really help *you* right now with the season you're in. Begin setting a regular time to get together with this friend, but don't let this time be just social. Confess that there's a growth area you're struggling with, talk about how you've seen God working in your friend's life, and ask for help with moving forward. As tough as the admission might be, it may take your relationship to a whole new level.

Form pairs, select the option you'd like to take on this week, and share your choice with your partner. Write what you plan to do in the space provided, and make plans to connect with your partner before the next session to check in and encourage each other. Take five minutes to do that now.

Walk It Out

☐ **...with my group** Take a hike together. Make it as easy or difficult as the physical condition of people in your group allows, but make sure there are a few turns (and better yet, different types of terrain and landmarks). Share a well-deserved snack or lunch when you reach your destination, and then have your group chew on these questions:

- If you were to describe to someone else how we got here, what would you say?
- How are some of the direction decisions we made like some of the challenges you've faced in your own life?
- If someone had wanted to turn back, what would you have said to help him or her keep going?
- How is all this like helping someone follow Jesus? How does sharing your experience help both you *and* them?
- Who could you help right now by sharing your experience?

...or think of your own!

Because I need others to help me grow in Jesus, too, I'll "Walk It Out" by:

____

____

____

____

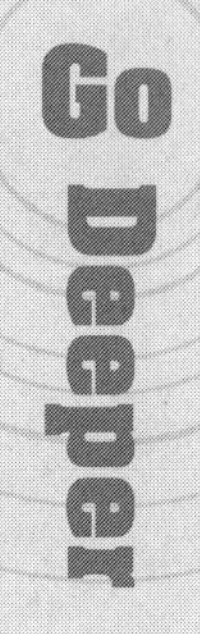

To dig deeper into the value of *being* mentored, here are some great resources:

Choose the Life: Exploring a Faith That Embraces Discipleship by Bill Hull (Baker)

Women Mentoring Women by Vickie Kraft and Gwynne Johnson (Moody)

Sacred Companions: The Gift of Spiritual Friendship and Direction by David G. Benner (InterVarsity)

Life Together: The Classic Exploration of Life in Community by Dietrich Bonhoeffer (HarperOne)

Transforming Discipleship: Making Disciples a Few at a Time by Greg Ogden (InterVarsity)

Gladly Accept Imitations

"*Imitate God, therefore, in everything you do, because you are his dear children. Live a life filled with love, following the example of Christ. He loved us and offered himself as a sacrifice for us, a pleasing aroma to God"* (EPHESIANS 5:1-2).

In this session, we'll journey...

from → **to**

seeing how we already affect others, knowingly or not... discovering how to model the growth we want to see in others.

Before gathering, make sure you have...

- ○ 2 pieces of paper for each person
- ○ a classical or jazz CD and something to play it on*

*See **Leader Notes**, page 169, for details.

Come and See

(about 20 minutes)

Have your music playing as people enter. For now, keep it at background level.

Give everyone a piece of paper.

» **I'm going to encourage you to do something you might very well have been told not to do back when you were in school: Take a minute to make your best paper airplane.**

Once people have finished their airplanes, have them line up on one side of your meeting area.

» **OK, when I say "go," let your planes fly. Go!**

Ask everyone to stand next to his or her plane. Have your groups identify which group member had the plane that flew the farthest. Then give everyone another sheet of paper.

» **Those of you whose planes went farthest: You're going to put on a little seminar for the rest of your group. Take a couple of minutes to teach your other group members how you made your vastly superior paper airplane.**

Everyone else: Follow your teacher's instructions, to the best of your abilities.

After two minutes, ask all the non-winners to line up and fly their new airplanes. Afterward, have them sit back down with their groups, and let the "teachers" lead the following discussion: →

Give subgroups five minutes to discuss, and then come back together. Share highlights and insights from your discussion.

◎ How did it feel to have me teach you how to make a paper airplane?

◎ How did my instructions help or hinder you?

◎ When has someone tried to teach you something you thought you already knew? How did you respond to that?

Come and See continued

» **We've had to do some moving around today, so let's take a minute or so to relax and collect our thoughts. Close your eyes, and simply listen to and enjoy the music that's playing. We'll pick our discussion back up after that.**

Turn up your music enough so everyone can enjoy it, but don't make it too loud. Once a minute or so has passed, discuss: →

You can turn off your music at this time or let it keep playing in the background; your call. Keep your music available for later, either way.

» **We communicate in a lot of different ways, don't we? Who we are and what we think comes through in a variety of ways—in our words, our actions, our facial expressions, our body language, and our tone of voice. Therefore, it's important that our message is consistent—not only so we're not sending mixed messages, but also so that what we communicate is consistent with what *God* wants to communicate.**

God will use us to bring change to other people's lives. But it comes at a personal cost. We have to be willing to get out of God's way and let God lead us. God may want us to open our mouths and spell things out to the people we're with. Or God may want us to keep our mouths shut and let others watch him work through us. We need to be ready to do both.

God will bring change into our lives, even as God uses us to bring change into other people's lives. Let's see what that might look like for each of us.

"*If we can't see our own lives changed by the power of the gospel, we have no right to expect to see the world changed by our message. If the gospel is not more important to us than life itself, the world will not be attracted to it. If they can't see that we value the gospel, why would we expect them to?*"

—Neil Cole, Search and Rescue: Becoming a Disciple Who Makes a Difference

◎ What do you think the people creating this music were thinking or feeling as they created it?

◎ How did the music express those thoughts or feelings without using any words?

◎ When has someone else "caught" what God has been doing in your life, whether you used words or not?

Seek and Find

(about 20 minutes)

Ask for a volunteer to read 1 Thessalonians 1:6-10, and then discuss →

» Let's reflect once more on our opening activities and on the different ways we can communicate what Jesus has shown us. Discuss these questions together: →

Encourage as many answers from the group as you can before going on to the next question. →

 **1 Thessalonians 1:6-10**

◎ How would you react if someone told you that you were imitating the Lord? Why?

◎ How did that imitation affect the Thessalonian Christian community? people outside the Thessalonian Christian community? Paul?

◎ What's easier for you personally: telling someone you know what Jesus has done in your life or walking out what Jesus is showing you and waiting for that person to ask you about it? Why?

◎ When and where are you most teachable? Why then? Explain your answers.

◎ How might the responses you've just heard affect how you approach the people you're invested in right now? Give specific examples.

Go

(about 20 minutes)

Ask for one or two volunteers to read Ephesians 5:1-2, 15-21.

» **We know that God can work through us, but there's also a command here. God's Word tells us to imitate God and, furthermore, that doing so is possible. Nobody's ever going to mistake us for Jesus, but Jesus wants us to be able to reflect his life so that others can see it. Let's spend a few more minutes on what might be keeping us from fully believing that.**

Get back into your groups and discuss the following questions. When you're done with your discussion, go right to Walk It Out. Let's come back together in 15 minutes.

"*The quickest way to the heart is through a wound.*"

—John Piper, Desiring God: Meditations of a Christian Hedonist

Ephesians 5:1-2, 15-21

◎ Describe a time in your life when you definitely weren't imitating God, a time you wish you could get a do over for.

◎ Think again about those people you're invested in now. What could you teach them so they don't repeat your mistakes?

◎ What has God shown you that you'd want others to imitate?

◎ What steps can you take to share the lessons you've learned—the good ones and the hard ones?

LEADER ▼

Walk It Out

(about 5 minutes)

›› The following options are here to help you put what you've learned into practice. But if God has prompted you to do something else through this session, then by all means do that!

GROUP ▼

I'll walk it out...

choose 1:

☐ ...as it comes

Whom do you encounter at least a few times a week but don't know particularly well? A co-worker from another department? The cashier at your local store? Your next-door neighbor? What's one thing you could do to model Jesus to that person, through your words, your actions, or both? Do it, and see where it takes you from there.

☐ ...with my family

Spend some extra time with a family member this week, and do something different together. Maybe your spouse is feeling a bit neglected, or your teenage son or daughter has been so on the go that you haven't connected in a while. Have an adventure together. Work together on a community project, or just take a long walk together and catch up. Find out what he or she has been dealing with lately, and find ways to bring Jesus into the situation, whether it's through prayer, counsel, or just being there.

☐ ...with my friends

Think back to your discussion in "Go." Is a friend facing a situation like the one you just discussed? What would you want him or her to know, based on what you discussed? Get together with that person this week, and communicate how God has helped you through your own struggles.

Form pairs, select the option you'd like to take on this week, and share your choice with your partner. Write what you plan to do in the space provided, and make plans to connect with your partner before the next session to check in and encourage each other. Take five minutes to do that now.

☐ **...with my group** What can you do as a group to, as the saying goes, "Show God's love in practical ways"? Pay to fill others' gas tanks? Give out food or beverages at a local event? Clean offices, roadsides, or even toilets? Think of a project your group could take on together, and do it. And if others ask why you're doing it, tell them.

...or think of your own!

Because I want to be an imitator of God, I'll "Walk It Out" by:

Walk It Out continued

Come back together as a group. Turn your music back on, if it's not still playing. Keep the volume fairly low. Ask people to take another minute to be silent and reflect once more on how they communicate Jesus to others—or would like to in the future.

prayer

After a minute has passed, lead your group in prayer. Ask God to reveal how each person can imitate God in the way God created him or her to do, and ask God to help each person be alert for opportunities to model the Christian life.

For those wanting to dig deeper into what it means to model Jesus to others, here are some great resources:

Group's BibleSense: Philippians: Sharing the Joy of Jesus (Group)

In His Steps by Charles Sheldon (Barbour)

Search and Rescue: Becoming a Disciple Who Makes a Difference by Neil Cole (Baker)

Connecting: The Mentoring Relationships You Need to Succeed by Paul D. Stanley and Robert Clinton (NavPress)

The Imitation of Christ by Thomas à Kempis (Hodder & Stoughton)

(Actively) Listen!

"And my message and my preaching were very plain. Rather than using clever and persuasive speeches, I relied only on the power of the Holy Spirit. I did this so you would trust not in human wisdom but in the power of God" (1 CORINTHIANS 2:4-5).

In this session, we'll journey...

from → seeing (and hearing) the importance of listening to God and others...

to giving more time and priority to our listening.

Before gathering, make sure you have...

- ○ nothing...just be there.

Be sure to check Leader Notes, page 171.

Come and See

(about 10 minutes)

» We're going to open this session in prayer, but we're going to do it a little differently today. Here's how we'll do it: Close your eyes, breathe out slowly, and pause for a moment when your lungs are empty. As you breathe out, talk silently to God. Tell God what's really on your heart right now. Then breathe back in slowly. When your lungs are full, stop and listen for God's answer.

We're going to take three minutes to do this, so just relax, focus on God, and silently share about your life and your cares. I'll let you know when it's time to stop.

"Mentoring is not about telling. It is about listening—to the Holy Spirit and to the life of the other... primarily about discernment and learning to recognize where God is already present and active in the heart of the other."

—*Keith R. Anderson and Randy D. Reese,* Spiritual Mentoring: A Guide for Seeking and Giving Direction

After three minutes, stop and invite people to share how God spoke to them during your silent prayer time. Then discuss the following:

» We started our time today by both talking to and listening to God. Hopefully during our brief prayer time, God shared something that you needed to hear—and you were able to hear because you stopped and listened.

Today we're going to consider how we can bring that same sense of expectancy into our discussions and relationships with others. Colossians 1:27 tells us that "Christ lives in you. This gives you assurance of sharing his glory." But how often do we stop to recognize that in other Christians—to listen for how God *is* already working in each of them?

To become a true spiritual friend to someone—and not just a friend who also happens to be a

◎ What was different for you about praying this way?

◎ How does taking the time to *listen* to God affect how you *talk* to God? Be specific.

Christian—we need to listen, to hear how God is working in those people we care about. And when we see God working in people's lives, we need to point it out to them because often the last person to see God working in us...is us.

Let's examine how we can become better listeners both with God and with those we care about.

Seek and Find

(about 30 minutes)

Ask for a volunteer to read 1 Corinthians 2:1-7. →

> *Seek first to understand, then to be understood.*
>
> —*Stephen R. Covey,* The 7 Habits of Highly Effective People

Have people get into their groups. Ask each group to designate a timekeeper.

» **You're going to try a different kind of listening now. Each of you think of a topic that gets you excited, whether that's something at church, a hobby, your family, or just something great that happened today or is about to happen. You'll each take two minutes to talk about that subject . There's just one catch: Before the next person speaks, he or she must summarize what the last person said, to that person's satisfaction.**

One more thing: The first person to talk has to recap the rules I've just stated, without looking in his or her book. The rest of the group: If that person didn't explain it correctly, read the instructions again until he or she gets it.

You can start whenever you're ready. When you're done, discuss these questions: →

After 15 minutes, come back together to share highlights and insights from your group discussion.

 **1 Corinthians 2:1-7**

- Paul talks here about how he approaches both mature Christians and not-so-mature Christians. What's the same and what's different about the ways he approaches these Christians?

- When has the Spirit told you, in essence, to just shut up and listen to someone else?

- Why do you think the Spirit held you back in that situation? What did both you and that other person discover through that time?

- How did this activity affect the way you spoke and listened to each other?
- How do you think your relationships would change if you did this level of listening all the time?

- How would this kind of listening make it easier to recognize how God is working in those you care about most?

Go

(about 20 minutes)

Ask for a volunteer to locate and get ready to read 1 Corinthians 2:9-16.

» **We're going to take one more opportunity to listen. This activity should be a little easier than the two we did earlier. Simply close your eyes and listen as** [your volunteer] **reads from 1 Corinthians.**

After your reading, discuss:

» **We'll get even deeper into those last couple of questions next week. But for now, we're going to "Walk It Out" a little differently this week. By this point in our season, you should know the person you're trying to develop a deeper spiritual friendship with. In your groups, discuss the following two questions together:**

- **What question would you want God to answer for that person right now?**
- **How might God use you to help him or her discover that answer?**

After your discussion, pray for one another. Bring what each of you has shared to God—now and after we leave here. Share as much as you're comfortable sharing with each other, and then pray together about what God has shown each of you. When you're done, you're free to quietly leave [or quietly hang out until everyone's finished, if you're in a small-group setting].

"Christians...forget that listening can be a greater service than speaking...[H]e who can no longer listen to his brother will soon be no longer listening to God either; he will be doing nothing but prattle in the presence of God too."

—Dietrich Bonhoeffer, Life Together

1 Corinthians 2:9-16

◎ How does listening to the Spirit help us listen to others? Give examples.

◎ What's the hardest thing about wanting to share something you believe the other person's not yet ready to hear?

◎ How can we prepare ourselves, and that other person, for the right opportunity to share it?

Because I need to listen to the people God wants me to help grow, I'll "Walk It Out" by:

____

____

____

____

____

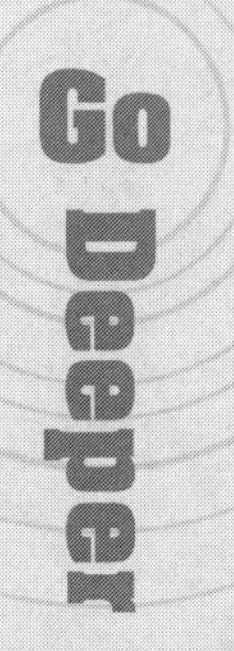

For those wanting to become better and more Christ-like listeners, here are some great resources:

God Space: Where Spiritual Conversations Happen Naturally by Doug Pollock (Group)

Listening for Heaven's Sake: Building Healthy Relationships With God, Self, and Others by Anne Clippard, David W. Ping, and Gary R. Sweeten (Equipping Ministries)

Spiritual Direction: Wisdom for the Long Walk of Faith by Henri J. M. Nouwen (HarperOne)

Holy Listening: The Art of Spiritual Direction by Margaret Guenther and Alan Jones (Cowley)

The Art of Christian Listening by Thomas N. Hart (Paulist)

How to Guide Without Steering

"So the Lord called a third time, and once more Samuel got up and went to Eli. 'Here I am. Did you call me?' Then Eli realized it was the Lord who was calling the boy. So he said to Samuel, 'Go and lie down again, and if someone calls again, say, 'Speak, Lord, your servant is listening.' So Samuel went back to bed" (1 SAMUEL 3:8-9).

In this session, we'll journey...

from understanding both our roles and our limitations in getting others where God wants them...

to identifying ways God can use us to help move others forward.

Before gathering, make sure you have...

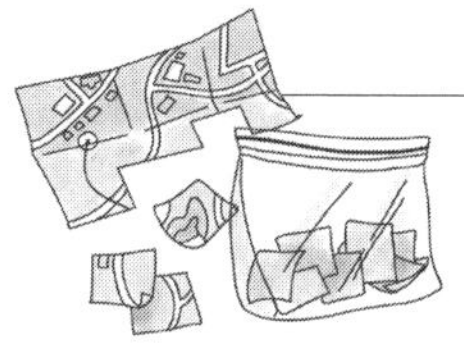

- a local street map, cut into about 25 equal-size pieces, for each group*

Optional activities (choose one or both):

- **Option A:** Discussion of Acts 10 in Go
- **Option B:** DVD of *Mr. Holland's Opus* (see page 85)

*See **Leader Notes**, page 171.

Come and See

(about 20 minutes)

Have people get into their groups. Give each group a cut-up map.

» **Your job is to work together to reassemble your map correctly. There's no race between groups here—take as much time as you need to get your maps right. Once you've succeeded, discuss these questions:** →

Gather everyone's attention after 15 minutes, keeping people in their groups. Have groups share highlights and insights from their discussion time.

"The trouble with life isn't that there is no answer, it's that there are so many answers."
—Ruth Benedict, cultural anthropologist

If possible, leave the reassembled maps out. You'll use them later.

» **We've just looked at times in our own lives when we thought or felt we had all the right information but somehow found ourselves off course. It's even more difficult to help others. We want to help; we think we know what will help. But even if we're right, we often don't help others by simply giving them answers.**

Sometimes we see what others need even more clearly than they do. And sometimes we really *don't* understand where God is trying to take them, and we project our own ideas and experiences onto them.

Either way, if *they* can't see where God is leading them, they might never get there. They could go the wrong way or do something without the conviction that it's truly God who's doing the leading. And without knowing that, they'll likely give up before they ever really get started.

The key is to get the people we care about to see for themselves where God is leading them. And God can use us to do that, whether we can see where God is leading them or not. Let's explore that.

◎ What was most difficult about piecing your map together? How did you figure out the right way to assemble it?

◎ When has a decision looked like "the right way" to you, yet turned out totally wrong (or at least unnecessary)?

◎ Looking back, why did you choose that route instead of another?

◎ What or who got you back on the right track? What did God teach you, as a result of that time?

Seek and Find

(about 20 minutes)

> *The extraordinary events of epiphany or revelation are few and rare, but the gentle or firm probing of a mentor's questions draw us back to the central action of spirituality:* to pay attention for the presence of God in everything.
>
> *—Keith R. Anderson and Randy D. Reese,* Spiritual Mentoring

» Let's spend some time now working on a different kind of puzzle. In your groups, read the Bible passages, and then discuss these questions: →

- 1 Samuel 3:1-10
- Matthew 7:1-6
- Galatians 6:1-5
- 2 Samuel 12:1-13
- John 16:5-15
- Titus 2:1-8

Bring everyone back together after 15 minutes, and share highlights and insights from your discussion time.

> *All too often we think it is our job to get people in a place where they can call on God, but what if God has already called them? Then our role in someone's life is to help them respond to the overtures of God.*
>
> *—Robert Gelinas,* Finding the Groove: Composing a Jazz-Shaped Faith

1 Samuel 3:1-10; 2 Samuel 12:1-13; Matthew 7:1-6; John 16:5-15; Galatians 6:1-5; Titus 2:1-8

◎ What elements of guidance do you see in each of these passages? What challenges do you see?

◎ Putting all of these passages together, what do you see as God's role in guiding others? What's our role?

◎ Think back to your map activity. How can we help people focus less on the pieces they don't understand and more on the ones they do? How will that help them figure out the rest of their "spiritual road maps"?

Go

(about 20 minutes)

If you've chosen **Option A**, *read on.*
If you're doing **Option B**, *go to page 85.*

Have one or more volunteers read Acts 10:1-23, 27-36, and 44-48. Then discuss →

> *To recognize an entry gate you do not ask, 'What are the problems in a person's life?' Instead you ask, 'What is this person struggling with in the midst of the situation?'*
>
> —*Paul David Tripp,* Instruments in the Redeemer's Hands

 **Acts 10:1-23, 27-36, 44-48**

◎ What's Peter struggling with here? How did God prepare both Cornelius and Peter, so that Peter could overcome it?

◎ Who has helped you overcome barriers you had created in your own head so you could do something you didn't think you were capable of? How did God prepare both you and that other person?

◎ How might God use you to help someone else get past a barrier this week?

LEADER ▼

Walk It Out

(about 5 minutes)

» **The following options are here to help you put what you've learned into practice. But if God has prompted you to do something else through this session, then by all means do that!**

GROUP ▼

I'll walk it out...

choose 1:

☐ ...as it comes

Sometimes guiding another person is as easy as asking, "What's God doing in your life?" So go ahead and ask someone this week. If you're talking with a not-yet Christian, consider asking this way: "When do believe you've encountered God?" The answers may surprise both of you.

☐ ...with my family

Is someone wrestling with a big decision right now? Take some time to help him or her work through it. Ask open-ended questions (ones to which there's no simple yes or no answer). Help that person articulate what he or she is thinking and feeling to better understand both. Be sparing with the advice. Let your family member discover his or her own answers, if possible. But be willing to share and "speak in" when you need to.

☐ ...with my friends

Try this one whether your friend is a Christian or, better yet, isn't. Take your friend out for coffee or lunch. OK, that's the easy part. But then ask, When have you felt the presence of God in your life? We won't guarantee that the answer won't be "never," but most of the time you'll get an answer that will completely take you by surprise. And you'll have created room to talk about God with that person in the future.

Form pairs, select the option you'd like to take on this week, and share your choice with your partner. Write what you plan to do in the space provided, and make plans to connect with your partner before the next session to check in and encourage each other. Take five minutes to do that now.

Walk It Out

☐ **...with my group** Do an affirmation time as a group. It could be part of a bigger event, such as a party, or a session unto itself. It's not unusual for others to see something you either can't see or won't admit to, even good things such as a spiritual gift, God's calling in a certain area, or just that you're a better person than you give yourself credit for. Take time to gather around each person and share how you see God working and what a blessing he or she is to you and to others. They'll remember it long after your time together.

...or think of your own!

Because I want to help others get where God wants them to go, I'll "Walk It Out" by:

____

____

____

____

____

____

____

Walk It Out continued

prayer

Come back together as a group. Ask everyone to hold a piece of the map the groups assembled at the beginning of your session as you lead in prayer. Ask God to reveal to each person how he or she might be used to guide someone else this week. Ask for God's wisdom to know when and how to talk and when to listen.

Have people take home their map pieces, as both a reminder of God's guidance in their lives and a reminder to let God use them to help guide others.

SEEING IT DIFFERENTLY

Go–Option B

LEADER Instead of the discussion of Acts 10, watch a scene from the movie *Mr. Holland's Opus*. Cue the movie to 30:30 (DVD Chapter 8), as Mr. Holland plays the piano. Stop the clip at 35:01, as Mr. Holland looks on admiringly.

GROUP

◎ What things did Mr. Holland do to get Miss Lang over her inability to play?

◎ Where do you see Mr. Holland getting over some of his own barriers to teaching as he helps Miss Lang?

◎ Who has helped you "play the sunset"? Who has gotten you over barriers you had created in your own head so you could do something you didn't think you were capable of? How did God prepare both you and that other person?

◎ How might God use you to help someone get past a barrier this week?

Go on to Walk It Out on page 82.

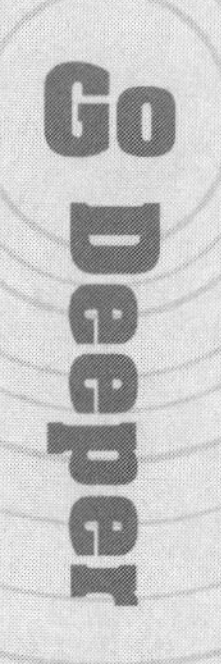

For those wanting to dig deeper into spiritual guidance, here are some great resources:

The Art of Spiritual Guidance by Carolyn Gratton (Crossroad)

Spiritual Direction and the Care of Souls: A Guide to Christian Approaches and Practices by Gary W. Moon and David G. Benner (InterVarsity)

Organic Disciplemaking: Mentoring Others Into Spiritual Maturity and Leadership by Dennis McCallum and Jessica Lowery (Touch)

Spiritual Mentoring: A Guide for Seeking and Giving Direction by Keith R. Anderson and Randy D. Reese (InterVarsity)

I *Don't* Understand... But I'm Not Leaving

"*Many of his disciples said, 'This is very hard to understand. How can anyone accept it?'...Simon Peter replied, 'Lord, to whom would we go? You have the words that give eternal life. We believe, and we know you are the Holy One of God'* " (JOHN 6:60, 68).

In this session, we'll journey...

from → **to**

understanding the importance of committing to even those we can't quite connect with...

seeing how God can use us no matter how much (or little) we have in common.

Before gathering, make sure you have...

- paper and pencils for everyone

See **Leader Notes**, page 172.

Come and See

(about 15 minutes)

» **Welcome, and thanks for coming. Get with your groups, and stay standing.**

As people group up, decide which group you'll single out for the activity that follows.

» **Every group but this one** [point to group]**, follow along with my clapping.**

Lead the other groups in a slow clap, at about marching speed. Once groups have picked up the beat and can carry it on their own—15 seconds is probably enough time to accomplish this—say something like, **Keep clapping as I give the other group its instructions.**

Turn your attention to your other group.

» **OK, I want you to begin clapping on the offbeat. When the other groups aren't clapping, that's where you come in. Let's begin.**

Lead the other group in clapping on the offbeat, as the other groups continue the main beat. After 15 more seconds, stop and give your groups a round of applause (yes, *more* clapping!). Have groups sit down and discuss these questions:

Gather everyone's attention after 10 minutes, keeping people in their groups. Have groups share highlights and insights from their discussion time.

» **It's easy to be there for people we naturally have things in common with. The people you're invested in right now might be among those people. Then again, you might be wondering why God put you with certain people. In either case, the answer is the same. God always wants us to push beyond the simply natural and into the spiritual so that our relationships can glorify God on every level.**

And the fact is, people we can't understand are not always the offbeat ones. We may be the ones who are "off"—at least to them. And that's OK, too. Some people

> *"Problems are only opportunities in work clothes."*
>
> *—Henry J. Kaiser, American industrialist*

◎ How easy or difficult was it to follow along once both groups were clapping? Why?

◎ When have you been the offbeat person in a group? What helped you find the group's "rhythm" (or did you)?

◎ Who's the most offbeat friend you've ever had? How has your friendship with that person influenced both of you?

truly are different; most, though, are simply different from us. The bigger point is, God puts people in our lives and sometimes we have a hard time getting in synch with them. But God is not letting us off the hook. God has put those people in our lives so he can grow them—and us—in a brand-new way.

The most important thing isn't that we totally click with others, but that we're willing to push forward and help other people discover how God is working in them. God wants to do what God wants to do. We need to be willing to show up and remain open to God's leading—even when we don't fully understand the other person or what God wants to do in him or her. The important thing is that God understands. And when we allow God into those relationships, we have something—and Someone—much greater in common with those people.

Seek and Find

(about 30 minutes)

Ask for a volunteer to read Acts 3:1-11, and then discuss:

Get back into your groups. Make sure everyone has paper and pencil.

» **We're going to pick on our offbeat group again. Would any groups care to come alongside and help them out?** (Pause for responses.)

Well, you're all going to get the chance to try to help them anyway.

Offbeat group: On your papers, each of you write an everyday problem that needs addressing, such as a car problem or a decision you need to make. It doesn't have to be something you're dealing with right now, just an everyday sort of problem.

Other groups: Among yourselves—and without knowing what the offbeat group's problems are—come up with one solution in your group. It could be "take two aspirin and call me in the morning" or something way more complex. Then write it down.

If possible, assign one "solution" group for each "problem" person. It's OK if more than one group gets assigned to a given person, though.

» **You'll have a minute to come up with your problems and solutions. Ready? Go!**

After a minute, ask a member of the offbeat group to share his or her problem, and then ask the corresponding group to share its solution. Once everyone has shared (and probably had a few good laughs), discuss the following together:

 **Acts 3:1-11**

◎ What would you have done in this situation, if you had been in Peter and John's place?

◎ Maybe we don't have the gift of healing, but how can we help others in ways they weren't asking for—in ways that actually *help*—even as we seek to understand their real issues?

◎ When have you felt totally unequipped to help someone else? How were you able to help anyway (or not)?

◎ When have *you* felt as though no one else—not even God—understood or could help you?

◎ Looking back, what do you wish you could have helped people understand (or understand more quickly)?

Go

(about 20 minutes)

» **Hebrews 4:15 tells us that Jesus understands our weaknesses because he faced the same testings we do. And Jesus not only understands us, he also understands the people we're with—for the same reasons he understands us.**

Jesus certainly understood his disciples. But did they understand him? Not so much. And yet, though they often dropped the ball, the disciples ultimately stuck it out with Jesus. And everyone in this room is a result of that faithfulness. Let's look at a couple of great examples of both their confusion and their faithfulness.

Read John 6:60-68 and John 11:7-16. Then discuss →

John 6:60-68, 11:7-16

◎ Where do you see both bewilderment and trust from the disciples here? How do you identify with Peter or Thomas?

◎ Let's think back to last week's session on guidance. How does putting the priority on what Jesus is trying to do, rather than our own understanding, help us help others? How does it grow us?

◎ How does sticking by someone, even when you can't understand what they're dealing with, *lead* to understanding?

LEADER ▼

Walk It Out

(about 5 minutes)

» **The following options are here to help you put what you've learned into practice. But if God has prompted you to do something else through this session, then by all means do that!**

GROUP ▼

I'll walk it out...

choose 1:

☐ ...as it comes

Who do you interact with regularly but just don't "get"? Set aside your discomfort, and reach out to that person this week. Start a conversation—even if you have to finish it, too. Take him or her out for coffee. Discover what you do have in common, and begin building on it.

☐ ...with my family

Who in your family totally bewilders you? You know who it is. Make time this week to just listen to this family member. Then take time to pray with him or her. *Really pray.* Pray with as much understanding as you have, and ask God to give each of you *more* understanding. And fully trust that God will provide it (James 1:5-6).

☐ ...with my friends

Who's your most offbeat friend right now? Enter into his or her world this week. Set a time to get with that person, but let him or her set the agenda for how you'll spend that time. (Use common sense, but give him or her permission to take you out of your comfort zone.) You'll learn more about that person, and maybe even discover you like that activity you'd been avoiding.

Form pairs, select the option you'd like to take on this week, and share your choice with your partner. Write what you plan to do in the space provided, and make plans to connect with your partner before the next session to check in and encourage each other. Take five minutes to do that now.

☐ **...with my group** If there's a church that worships differently from yours—because of its doctrine, tradition, or size—go as a group to check it out. Don't go to analyze or critique (let alone criticize) how people in that church do things, but go seeking to understand and worship alongside other members of the body of Christ. You just might discover something you'll want to add to your own worship time.

...or think of your own!

Because I need to commit even when I don't understand, I'll "Walk It Out" by:

____

____

____

____

____

____

____

Walk It Out continued

prayer➔ Come back together as a group. Ask God's help in committing to the offbeat people God has put in your life. Ask God to reveal ways you can commit to and become better friends with them, even as you work on understanding them better. Ask for humility to understand how God wants to use these people to enrich your life as well—maybe far more than you enrich theirs.

For those wanting to dig deeper into moving from not understanding to understanding others, here are some great resources:

God Space: Where Spiritual Conversations Happen Naturally by Doug Pollock (Group)

Finding the Groove: Composing a Jazz-Shaped Faith by Robert Gelinas (Zondervan)

Consuming Love: Commitment, Friendship and Passion, What It Means to Be Connected to God's Heart by Steve Harrison (Destiny Image)

Simple Spirituality: Learning to See God in a Broken World by Christopher L. Heuertz (InterVarsity)

Getting Unstuck

"*May you experience the love of Christ, though it is too great to understand fully. Then you will be made complete with all the fullness of life and power that comes from God. Now all glory to God, who is able, through his mighty power at work within us, to accomplish infinitely more than we might ask or think*" (EPHESIANS 3:19-20).

In this session, we'll journey...

from → **to**

exploring how to help others recognize their own blind spots...

taking the next steps in becoming the people God has created all of us to be.

Before gathering, make sure you have...

- ○ at least 1 straight-back chair for each group
- ○ a newsprint tablet, blackboard, or white board

See **Leader Notes**, page 172.

Come and See

(about 15 minutes)

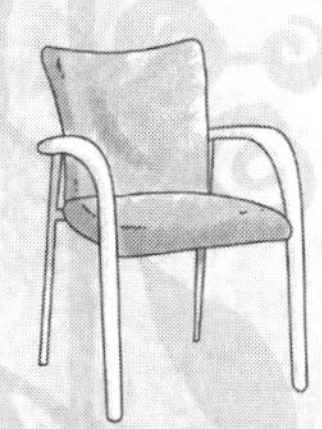

Stand up and ask people to get into their groups. Remain standing, and have a chair nearby.

Ask for a volunteer to sit in your chair. Stand behind your volunteer, and tell him or her:

» **Please close your eyes. I'm going to snap my fingers. As I do, I want you to point to where the sound is coming from.**

"Growth is often painful and scary. There is no growth without change; there is no change without fear or loss; and there is no loss without pain. Every change involves a loss of some kind: You must let go of old ways in order to experience the new."

—Rick Warren, The Purpose-Driven Life

Imagine an arc over your volunteer's head, lining up directly between his or her ears, starting at the nose and ending at the nape of the neck. Snap your fingers several times in various places along that arc, at least two feet from the person's head. After each snap, ask him or her to point to where the snap came from. After several snaps, ask your volunteer to open his or her eyes, and ask the rest of the group how he or she did.

» **Now try the same thing in your groups. Let everyone have a turn snapping and a turn sitting. After each turn, talk about how each person did. When everyone has had a turn, discuss these questions:**

Allow 10 minutes, and then come back together. Share highlights and insights from your discussion time.

» **Almost all of us all have had blind spots in our lives that God has unveiled to us, and in many cases God has used others who care about us to reveal those things. It may have been a wonderful aha moment for**

◎ What, if anything, helped you figure out where the snapping was coming from?

◎ Where were your biggest "blind spots"—those places where you had no idea where the sound was coming from?

◎ Think of a blind spot that's been uncovered in your own life—something good or bad that you were incapable of seeing. What (or who) helped you finally discover it? Why do you think it stayed hidden for so long?

us when the light suddenly came on. On the other hand, it may have been painful or even made us angry at first, but once we got past our reactions, we realized that the other person had done us a huge favor.

We're going to look at how God can use us to become those catalysts for others. Perhaps the most critical role in growing others is getting them past their blind spots so they can see the people God has created them to be and finally get on with becoming that person. So let's jump in.

Seek and Find

(about 35 minutes)

So, as Jesus' current assistants in his ongoing program, one important way of characterizing our work of 'training disciples to do everything I told you' is 'bringing them to actually believe all the things they have already heard.'

—*Dallas Willard,* The Divine Conspiracy

» Let's reflect again on those times God has opened our eyes and brought change into our lives.

Write down everyone's responses on your white board, thanking them for their contributions as you do so. Then continue your discussion:

» God will use anything and anyone to get through to us. In many cases, the biggest blind spot any of us has is the inability to grasp how much God loves us. But the truth is, God is cheering us on. *God* is pushing us forward. And God is committed to helping us overcome every obstacle we face—even when that obstacle is us. God doesn't have our limits, and he wants our trust to empower us to overcome our limits. More to the point, God wants us to overcome the limits we've put on ourselves, limits God never intended to be there.

So let's look at how God sees us—the people we already are, whether we fully believe it or not—so we can help others see it, too. Get back into your groups, read the Bible passages below, and then discuss the question that follows.

- Romans 8:31-39
- Ephesians 2:4-10
- 2 Peter 1:3-9
- 1 John 3:1-3

After 10 minutes, bring everyone back together. Encourage people to share highlights and insights from their discussion time.

Ask for a volunteer to read Romans 8:26-28.

» Put this passage together with the passages and discussions we've just had, and let's discuss this question:

We've looked at the bad decisions in our lives and then asserted to God, 'You could really use this stuff!' That's the hope in the tragedy of confession. That we serve a God who actually can—and does—redeem everything, even our sin.

—*Robert Gelinas,* Finding the Groove: Composing a Jazz-Shaped Faith

◎ What are some of the approaches—or strategies, if you can call them that—that God has used and that others have used *with* you as they were led by God?

◎ Let's look at our list. Why do you think there's such a variety here?

Romans 8:31-39; Ephesians 2:4-10; 2 Peter 1:3-9; 1 John 3:1-3

◎ Answer the following both scripturally and experientially: Who are you in Jesus? In other words: What does God tell you through the Word, and what has God *shown* you about the person he's created you to be?

Romans 8:26-28

◎ How does understanding how God sees us, and knowing God uses *whatever* we give him to work with, help us move past anything we're facing in life right now?

Go

(about 10 minutes)

Ask for a volunteer to read Ephesians 3:14-21, then discuss: ⟶

» **This season is focused on helping others grow into the people God has created them to be, just as God has already grown us. But we're always growing, too. There are always new challenges we need to face and allow God (and others) to help us through. And sometimes things we had thought we'd overcome come back to haunt us in a different way. There's a good chance you're facing a situation right now where you're wondering what God wants you to do next.**

Therefore, let's take a step back. Take a minute to reflect: Is there an area where you're having problems continuing in Christ's love right now? Let's take time now to prepare ourselves so God can better use us to prepare those we care about as well.

Instead of our regular "Walk It Out" time, I'm going to lead us in prayer. After that, you're free either to leave or to get with the people in your groups and further talk through the things we're going to pray over silently right now. You've been together a couple of months now. Don't be afraid to take the time to open up and speak into each other's lives, if that's what needs to happen today, or to be there for those who need to hear from you.

Let's pray.

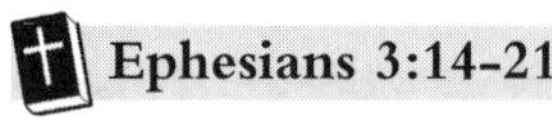

Ephesians 3:14-21

◎ How can seeing and remembering God's love and power in your life help free others to see it in their lives?

Because God wants me to be an agent for change, in others' lives *and* in my own, I'll "Walk It Out" by:

Go continued

prayer

» **Lord, we're willing to change. Change us as you need to. If we're in the right place right now and we just need to see that, show us. If we're not, show us our blind spots. Use those people we care about to help us see your work.**

Lord, guide us. Help us to only take on what you want us to take on. Help us to see everything as an opportunity for growth, no matter what the earthly outcome is.

You love those we love far more than we can even love them. Help us see that their lives are already in your hands. Use us as you see fit. Help us let go when it's your turn to work. As we just read in Ephesians, help us each to experience the love of Jesus, even though we can't understand how truly great that is. But begin to complete us in all the fullness of your life and power. And help us trust that your mighty power can work within and through us to accomplish infinitely more than we might ask or think.

Lord, help us trust you with every part of our lives, and help us love others the way Jesus did—and does. Amen.

Encourage people once more to spend time in their groups, if God has been speaking to them about specific issues during your prayer time. Remain available if anyone wants to talk one-on-one or needs further prayer.

For those wanting to camp out and dig deeper into how to help others see who they are in Jesus and move forward, here are some great resources:

Celebrate Recovery by John Baker (Zondervan)

Breaking Free: Discover the Victory of Total Surrender by Beth Moore (B&H)

The Wounded Healer: Ministry in Contemporary Society by Henri Nouwen (Image)

Instruments in the Redeemer's Hands: People in Need of Change Helping People in Need of Change by Paul David Tripp (P & R Publishing)

Help! (or, You Can't Do It Alone, Part II)

"*Dear brothers and sisters, if another believer is overcome by some sin, you who are godly should gently and humbly help that person back onto the right path. And be careful not to fall into the same temptation yourself"* (GALATIANS 6:1).

In this session, we'll journey...

from recognizing when we're in over our heads trying to help others...

to understanding when it's time to refer others for more specialized help.

Before gathering, make sure you have...

○ no supplies...just *be* there.

That said, *please* read the **Leader Notes** on page 173 before this session.

Optional activities (choose one or both):

You have two options for using the movie clip this week. Look over this session, and decide what sequence will work best for you and your group.

○ **Option A #1:** The trust-fall activity in Come and See (see page 108)

○ **Option A #2:** The opening discussion of Matthew and Galatians in Seek and Find (see page 110)

○ **Option B:** DVD of *Walk the Line* (see page 116)

Come and See

(about 10 minutes)

If you've chosen **Option A** *#1, read on.*
If you're doing **Option B** *at this point, go to page 116.*

Ask people to get into their groups.

» **If there are two or four people in your group, pair off, and have the larger person in each pair stand in front while the smaller person stands about three feet behind. If there are three people in your group, have two stand in front while the third person stands behind them.**

Give everyone a few moments to get into position.

» **Those in front: Make your bodies stiff, and prepare to fall backward into the person behind you. But don't do it yet.**

Those in back: Be prepared to catch your partner(s). (Pause.)

If you haven't read the Leader Notes yet, stop and read the first bullet point *now*, before going any further.

Ask everyone to sit down to discuss the following questions as a larger group: →

» **All of us have faced situations that were too much for one person to handle—where we were completely unequipped to find solutions. It's even harder when those situations involve someone we care about. Even if you've somehow managed to not face this kind of situation with a friend or family member, chances are you will at some point in your life.**

And the advice here is not to bail when things get tough, but to acknowledge that the situation is something more than you can handle. Your role at that point is to help that person get the help he or she needs—even as you do what you can do as a friend. Let's explore what that might look like.

◎ What was going through your head as you waited, either to catch your partner or to be caught? Why?

◎ When have you been in a situation when too much was falling on you? How did you deal with it? What did you learn from it?

Seek and Find

(about 35 minutes)

If you've chosen **Option A** *#2, read on.*
If you're doing **Option B**, *go to page 116.*

Ask for volunteers to read Matthew 18:15-20 and Galatians 6:1-5.

> *Hence, you must know when, how, and to whom you must say 'no.' This involves considerable difficulty at times. You must not hurt people, or want to hurt them, yet you must not placate them at the price of infidelity to higher and more essential values.*
>
> —*Thomas Merton,* Conjectures of a Guilty Bystander

» **The passages we just read tell us specifically how to deal with those caught up in sin, and that might be the kind of situation we're talking about. But let's expand our scope here. People don't become trapped or paralyzed only when they're caught up in sin. It can happen when they're *victims* of sin. It can happen when they're overwhelmed by the results of an imperfect world—a death in the family, a long-term problem another family member is caught up in and can't handle, or hurts they've experienced because of messy situations such as layoffs at work or a church split—and they just can't seem to get past them.**

We're not here to discuss at what speed people should or shouldn't recover—simply what our roles should or shouldn't be in that recovery process.

So with this broader definition in mind, let's put these passages together and discuss: →

Encourage everyone to think of actions in addition to those suggested in these passages.

 **Matthew 18:15-20; Galatians 6:1-5**

◎ What attitude should we have toward others who have "fallen and can't get up"?

◎ What actions might we have to put with those attitudes, depending on the situation?

Seek and Find continued

» **As we discussed last week, we want to help people get unstuck. But we also need to remember that it's never entirely up to us. It's ultimately the Spirit's job. Indeed, the Spirit has gifted others to do what we can't. Others have resources and wisdom beyond what we can give. We need to recognize when it's time to let go of our need to be the one who "fixes" those we care about—or enables them to continue in the behaviors they need to get out of. Since we're dealing with a hard subject here, let's discuss a few hard questions.** →

Let's take our scenarios one step further. Let's say you knew someone who could help your friend—your pastor, a counselor, a program—someone who had the time or skills or resources you lacked. Let's talk about what that would look like. →

◎ Name a situation people face where friendship might not be enough to get them through.

◎ Put yourself in the situation you just described or thought of. When would you know you were in over your head? What would the other person need that you *know* you can't give?

◎ Truthfully, what feelings would you have about "letting go" and letting that other person take over—not surrendering your love or friendship, but letting go of those responsibilities you'd been trying to carry? Why?

◎ What else would have to change in your relationship with your friend once you had let go of those responsibilities? Explain.

Go

(about 20 minutes)

Ask for a volunteer to read 2 Corinthians 2:5-11.

Then ask for volunteers to share about a time they *did* have to let go of their need to "fix" or enable another person, or a time they had to direct someone to the specific help the person needed. Share as many stories as you can fit in 10 minutes (unless you have time to go longer).

» **Instead of selecting from the regular Walk It Out options, get back into your groups. If there's someone in particular who has come to mind today during our session, talk about him or her—as much as you're comfortable doing. Take the time to pray together for those people, and pray that God would give each of you the wisdom and compassion to know how to hand over responsibility when necessary, without letting go of your friendship.**

Take as much time as you need. When you're done, you're free to quietly leave [or quietly hang out until everyone's finished, if you're in a small-group setting]**.**

Because sometimes the best way to help is to realize how much I *can't* help, I'll "Walk It Out" by:

SEEING IT DIFFERENTLY

Come and See/Seek and Find–Option B

LEADER Instead of the trust-fall activity—or in place of the discussion of Matthew and Galatians that opens Seek and Find—watch a scene from the movie *Walk the Line*. This scene portrays Johnny Cash trying to kick his drug addiction and facing the demons that drove him there, especially the tragic death of his older brother when he was a child. Cue the movie to 1:46:19 (DVD Chapter 29), as June calls out "John?" Stop the clip at 1:52:38, as Johnny and June enter church.

Note: This scene contains a few expletives as Ezra Carter pulls his rifle on the drug dealer trying to visit Johnny's house. There are a couple of ways to deal with this. You can either stop the video at 1:48:40, as Johnny slumps down, and jump to 1:49:08, just after said expletives and as the dealer is being chased back into his truck. Or you can simply mute the scene from 1:49:03, as the dealer arrives on Johnny's deck, and bring back the sound at 1:49:08.

GROUP

- Why do you think the Carter family decided to help Johnny to this degree? What do you think motivated their kindness and commitment to him?

- What did you think about Mother Maybelle's comment to June, "You're *already* down there?" What did she mean?

- Be honest: Would you have been able to make the kind of hardcore commitment the Carter family made to Johnny? (And if you have, please share about it, if you're comfortable doing so.) Where would you have drawn the line?

If you use this scene in Come and See, pick up at the statement which begins, **"All of us have faced situations…"** If you use this during Seek and Find, pick up at the statement beginning, **"As we discussed last week, we want to help people get unstuck."**

For those wanting to dig deeper into when to help and when to *get* help, here are some great resources:

Group's Emergency Response Handbook series (Group)

Boundaries: When to Say Yes, When to Say No, to Take Control of Your Life by Henry Cloud and John Townsend (Zondervan)

When Someone Asks for Help: A Practical Guide for Counseling by Everett L. Worthington (InterVarsity)

Why Do Christians Shoot Their Wounded?: Helping (Not Hurting) Those With Emotional Difficulties by Dwight L. Carlson (InterVarsity)

Should I Stay or Should I Go?

"*You didn't choose me. I chose you. I appointed you to go and produce lasting fruit, so that the Father will give you whatever you ask for, using my name*" (JOHN 15:16).

In this session, we'll journey...

from realizing when it's time to let others take their next steps, even if it's away from *us*...

to discovering God's perspective so we can celebrate when it happens.

Before gathering, make sure you have...

Optional activities (choose one or both):

Seek and Find

- ○ **Option A:** Discussion of Mark 5:1-20
- ○ **Option B:** DVD of *Star Wars: Episode IV–A New Hope* (see page 129)

Go

- ○ **Option A:** Discussion of Jesus letting his disciples go
- ○ **Option B:** Another scene from *Star Wars* (see page 130)

See **Leader Notes**, page 174.

Come and See

(about 15 minutes)

Have people get into their groups.

» Take a few moments to pick a representative from each of your groups. Once you've all made your selections, I'll tell you what to do next.

Allow up to 30 seconds for groups to choose, and then regain everyone's attention. Ask each group's representative to stand, and then ask those standing to count off—the first group's representative is 1, the second group's representative is 2, and so on. Point to your first representative to get things started, then direct as needed.

» I'm going to ask our representatives to do something they haven't had to do this entire season—leave your groups.

Join the next group in our sequence—the representative from Group 1 will go to Group 2, and so on. The last person in our sequence will join the first group. Go ahead and switch.

Give people time to regroup.

» Now in your new groups, discuss these questions:

Allow 10 minutes for discussion, and then come back together to share highlights and insights from your discussion time.

> *"Human love breeds hothouse flowers; spiritual love creates the fruits that grow healthily in accord with God's good will in the rain and storm and sunshine of God's outdoors."*
>
> *—Dietrich Bonhoeffer,* Life Together

» In our last session, we explored times we need to let go and let others help. In this session, we'll look at a different kind of letting go. It's the letting go that has to happen when the person you've been pouring your life into is growing and ready to get on with what God has for him or her, *and you have to step aside and let it happen.*

It might not even require that you see less of that person, but you know there's been a shift in the relationship—and you have to let that person take those next steps on his or her own. You know it's a good

◎ Share about a time one of your children started kindergarten or college or moved out. If you don't have kids, share about your own experience leaving for school or leaving home and how your parents reacted.

◎ How did that experience change the way you saw your child (or parent)?

thing, but it can still be painful to let someone you love and have shared life with move forward without you.

And let's not forget: It's tough for the other person, too. It's not easy to give up the safety of a spiritual friendship—the security of relying and depending upon someone you know is there for you—and venture into the unknown. And if you're on that side of the equation, the good news is you're bringing the best part of the other person with you as you head forward.

Sometimes you'll be the one who initiates that change; sometimes it will be the other person. But when that time comes, hopefully you'll both recognize it for what it is and take joy in it, despite the sadness that comes along with letting go. So today we're going to examine what that time of transition might look like and how we can make that time as joyful and beneficial as possible for both sides.

Seek and Find

(about 20 minutes)

If you've chosen **Option A**, *read on.*
If you're doing **Option B**, *go to page 129.*

Ask for a volunteer to read Mark 5:1-20, and then discuss: →

"We are prevented from following in another's footsteps and are called to an incomparable association with Christ. The Bible makes it clear that every time that there is a story of faith, it is completely original"

—Eugene Peterson, **Run With the Horses**

» Now that we're a ways into this session, it's OK to tell you that you'll be getting back into your original groups before we go to Walk It Out. You've come too far together to be separated now. But before we do that, get back into your new groups to discuss these questions: →

Allow 10 minutes for discussion, and then come back together to share highlights and insights from your discussion time.

Mark 5:1-20

◎ What things wouldn't have happened if Jesus had agreed to let the (formerly) demon-possessed man come with him?

◎ Your own example probably isn't as dramatic as the one in Mark, but when have you had to step aside so someone could take a positive step forward?

◎ What results did you see from that letting go?

◎ How did the changes we made today affect your group dynamic?

◎ What does that tell you about the difficulties of letting go and moving on, for both those who stayed with the group and those who left?

Go

(about 25 minutes)

If you've chosen **Option A**, *read on.*
If you're doing **Option B**, *go to page 130.*

» Let's look at an example of Jesus letting others—his own disciples—go. As we read and listen, think again about Jesus' own context here. He's not only about to leave his disciples; he knows he's hours away from being arrested, tortured, and crucified. And he knows what his disciples are about to face as well. And yet… well, let's see what "yet" looks like.

Ask for volunteers to read John 15:11-16, 15:26–16:7, and 16:32-33, and then discuss: →

» Take a minute to read the quote by Neil Cole, and then we'll discuss two more questions. →

Remind people to rejoin their original groups, and then go on to Walk It Out.

John 15:11-16, 15:26–16:7; 16:32-33

◎ What's changing in Jesus' relationship with his disciples here? Name as many things as you can.

◎ What's Jesus' attitude? Why?

◎ How does knowing that Jesus chose to free us—but that we're still connected to him no matter what—help us become who God has created us to be?

◎ How does knowing this help us stay connected to those *we* might need to let go of?

◎ How can we encourage and celebrate with those who are ready to take the "final exam" and graduate? How has each of you made this moment possible?

> *"Simply making disciples is not enough; your disciples must also make disciples, or the commission has not been accomplished. In a very real sense, your final exam is not to be taken by you, but by another person."*
>
> —*Neil Cole,* Search and Rescue: Becoming a Disciple Who Makes a Difference

LEADER ▼

Walk It Out

(about 5 minutes)

» The following options are here to help you put what you've learned into practice. But if God has prompted you to do something else through this session, then by all means do that!

GROUP ▼

I'll walk it out...

choose 1:

☐ ...as it comes

Think about how the principle of letting go applies to other circumstances in your life. What other changes—changes that, if made, would honor God—have you been hesitating to make at your work or other more informal relationships? What will those changes mean for you and for the people those changes affect? Think it through, settle on it, and then do it!

☐ ...with my family

Is someone in your family in one of the stages we discussed in Come and See? Or is it you who's about to make a decision that's going to greatly affect the rest of your family? Sit down with your family this week, and lay everything on the table—your thoughts, your feelings, and how much you love and are proud of them, even as you're dealing with those changes together.

☐ ...with my friends

Do you have a friendship in major transition right now—an upcoming move, a change in responsibilities or time commitment? Or as we've focused on today, is God calling one of you to something brand-new? Change isn't bad, but some changes are easier to deal with than others. Spend some time together celebrating your friendship, what God has done with it, what God is going to do with each of you next, and how you can keep your friendship growing under your new circumstances.

Form pairs, select the option you'd like to take on this week, and share your choice with your partner. Write what you plan to do in the space provided, and make plans to connect with your partner before the next session to check in and encourage each other. Take five minutes to do that now.

☐ **...with my group** You've only got three weeks left in this season; what are you going to do next? Here's one thing you definitely should do: Party! Whether you're staying together as a group after this season or moving on, take the time to celebrate what God has done among you over the last few months. Start planning now. And as a group, think about what you want to share and celebrate!

...or think of your own!

Because walking it out sometimes means letting *others* take the next steps, I'll "Walk It Out" by:

Walk It Out continued

prayer Come back together as a group. Thank God for change and for growth. Ask for help in recognizing those people who are ready to move forward and what your roles are in helping them. Ask God to help you let go and let God carry them where they need to go, and ask God to help you fully share in his joy when that happens.

To dig deeper into how to help others take their own next steps, here are some great resources:

Becoming a Woman of Influence: Making a Lasting Impact on Others by Carol Kent (NavPress)

Spiritual Fathers: Restoring the Reproductive Church by Dan Schaffer (Building Brothers)

The Heart of Mentoring: Ten Proven Principles for Developing People to Their Fullest Potential by David A. Stoddard (NavPress)

Spiritual Mentoring: A Guide for Seeking and Giving Direction by Keith R. Anderson and Randy D. Reese (InterVarsity)

SEEING IT DIFFERENTLY

Seek and Find–Option A

LEADER Instead of reading and discussing Mark 5 during "Seek and Find," watch a scene from the movie *Star Wars: Episode IV—A New Hope* (the original 1977 movie). A big theme of the movie is Luke Skywalker's apprenticeship to Ben Obi-Wan Kenobi. This scene represents a major change to that relationship, as Obi-Wan confronts a former apprentice gone terribly wrong, Darth Vader. Cue the movie to 1:29:53 (DVD Chapter 38), as Obi-Wan confronts Darth Vader. Stop the clip at 1:32:26, as Luke screams "No!" Then have groups discuss:

GROUP

◎ When have you had to step aside so someone else could take a positive step forward?

◎ Were you able to let go as peacefully as Obi-Wan Kenobi did, or did it feel like you'd been repeatedly run through with a light sabre? And for that matter, did the other person scream "No!" (at least figuratively)? Explain.

Pick up at the leader statement on page 122, beginning, **Now that we're a ways into this session...**

SEEING IT DIFFERENTLY

Go–Option B

LEADER Start Go with another scene from *Star Wars*. Cue the movie to 1:55:29 (DVD Chapter 47), as Luke is adjusting his targeting computer. Stop the clip at 1:57:29, after Obi-Wan says, "Remember, the Force will be with you, always." Then discuss the following questions:

GROUP

◎ How was Obi-Wan's influence felt throughout this scene, even though it was a task only Luke could complete?

Ask for volunteers to read John 15:11-16, 15:26–16:7, and 16:32-33, then discuss the next question:

GROUP

◎ How does knowing we're always connected to Jesus, no matter what, help us stay connected to those *we* might need to let go of?

Pick up at the discussion of the Neil Cole quote on page 124.

Remaining as You Go

"*But if you remain in me and my words remain in you, you may ask for anything you want, and it will be granted! When you produce much fruit, you are my true disciples. This brings great glory to my Father"* (JOHN 15:7-8).

In this session, we'll journey...

from realizing that we need to be refilled, especially as we give more to others...

to identifying how we can become even more deeply connected to Jesus.

Before gathering, make sure you have...

- ice cream and a wide variety of toppings*

*See **Leader Notes**, page 174, for details.

Come and See

(about 10 minutes)

» We've covered a lot of tough stuff in the last few sessions, so let's kick back a little this week before we get down to business. Go grab a bowl of ice cream—and while you're at it, go wild with the toppings (or at least as wild as you want to go)! Once you've loaded up, sit down with your groups, and as you enjoy your ice cream, discuss the following:

After five minutes, come back together as a larger group.

» We've spent the last few months exploring how Jesus can use us to pour our lives into others around us and help them move deeper into what God is calling them to. But as we do that, it becomes even more important for us to stay connected to Jesus. Even when things go well, our commitments can be demanding and even draining—physically, mentally, emotionally, and certainly spiritually. We need to keep our focus and go even deeper with Jesus so we can continue to draw on his strength. Let's examine how we can keep doing that.

"When you deal with externals, what you are really doing is driving your soul farther outward from your spirit. The more your spirit is focused on these outward things, the farther it is removed from its center and its resting place!"

—Jeanne Guyon, Experiencing the Depths of Jesus Christ

◎ Why did you pick the toppings you did? How would other toppings have affected the taste of your ice cream? Be descriptive.

◎ What's going on in your life right now that you wish wasn't so difficult or complex—where you wish there were a few less "toppings" piled on?

Seek and Find

(about 30 minutes)

Ask for a volunteer to read John 15:1-8. Then discuss: ⟶

[W]e strive for bare minimums instead of pursuing what is truly possible, namely, unending, unbroken communion with Jesus. We were designed to live with God for all time, for God is with us all of the time. But when time has us, grace is suffocated.

—Robert Gelinas, Finding the Groove: Composing a Jazz-Shaped Faith

» Let's take this idea of remaining and see how it applied to Jesus' disciples 2,000 years ago. We've probably read these passages in the past and marveled at Jesus' followers, and not in a good way. How could they have missed so much when Jesus was right there in front of them? But if we're honest and believe what Jesus tells us, we're guilty of the exact same things. So let's move past our own "dullness of heart" and look at both sides of these passages.

 **John 15:1-8**

◎ What steps to growth, as it were, do you see in this passage?

◎ What things—even good things—can pull us away from Jesus?

◎ At what point do you usually realize you've stopped "remaining"? Why then?

Seek and Find continued

Ask people to get back into their groups. Assign Luke 24:13-35 to half of the groups and John 20:11-18 to the other half. Read, and then discuss the following questions: ⟶

After 15 minutes, bring everyone back together, and share highlights and insights from your discussion time.

Luke 24:13-35; John 20:11-18

◎ Why do you think the people in your passage couldn't see Jesus?

◎ Nonetheless, what things had they done to stay connected to Jesus so they would be ready to see him?

◎ When has Jesus prepared you to see him more clearly, even if you didn't know it at the time?

◎ How did staying connected to Jesus—even if you didn't *feel* connected—help you get through that time?

Go

(about 20 minutes)

Ask for volunteers to read Psalm 19, Philippians 4:8-9, and Hebrews 4:9-16. Then discuss these questions: →

"Certainly the discipline of creating time for reflection is a lifeline for spiritual health. Without times in quiet, thoughtful reflection, our spirituality remains shallow, anemic and misguided."

—Keith R. Anderson and Randy D. Reese, Spiritual Mentoring: A Guide for Seeking and Giving Direction

"And the renewal of worship keeps the glow and power of our true homeland an active agent in all parts of our being. To 'hear and do' in the atmosphere of worship is the clearest, most obvious and natural thing imaginable."

—Dallas Willard, The Divine Conspiracy

Psalm 19; Philippians 4:8-9; Hebrews 4:9-16

◎ What different ways of staying connected with Jesus do you find in these passages?

◎ Which of these come easiest to you? Which don't?

◎ How can we bring these Christ-connections more into our daily lives and into our worship time together?

LEADER ▼

Walk It Out

(about 5 minutes)

» The following options are here to help you put what you've learned into practice. But if God has prompted you to do something else through this session, then by all means do that!

GROUP ▼

I'll walk it out...

choose 1:

☐ ...as it comes

Walk it out literally this week: Take your own personal "walk to Emmaus." Take an extended period of time to take a walk on your own, pouring out what you're feeling to Jesus. Put it all out there so that Jesus has room to deal with your own dullness of heart and help you see past your hurts and struggling—and see him instead.

☐ ...with my family

Do you have a regular devotional time with your family? Start one, or change it up. Use your time in God's Word as a catalyst to see how God is working in your lives, rather than as a task to complete. Make most of your time about sharing what God is doing or trying to do in your lives.

☐ ...with my friends

Here's a different approach toward your time together. Instead of focusing on sharing about your own lives or on pushing each other forward (good things, but...), spend some time this week each sharing how you're seeing God work in the other person. You may very well point out things to one another that you're too close to see for yourselves.

Form pairs, select the option you'd like to take on this week, and share your choice with your partner. Write what you plan to do in the space provided, and make plans to connect with your partner before the next session to check in and encourage each other. Take five minutes to do that now.

☐ **...with my group** Take a retreat as a group, and get more connected with Jesus and each other. Set aside a large chunk of time—you should have at least an hour of pure alone time. After your time alone with God, gather back together to share what you experienced during your time of sacred solitude. Also discuss how you can make a more regular time of this, both individually and as a group.

...or think of your own!

Because the more I'm connected to Jesus the better I can connect to others, I'll "Walk It Out" by:

____

____

____

____

____

____

____

Walk It Out continued

prayer➲ Come back together as a group. Ask people to bow their heads quietly while you re-read John 15:1-8 aloud. Ask everyone to quietly consider how to connect more consistently with Jesus. Allow two minutes for quiet reflection and prayer afterward.

Close your time together by asking God to help people see how Jesus is already present with them, no matter what they're facing or how distracted they've let themselves get. Ask God to reveal to each person how he or she can remain more deeply in Jesus.

To dig deeper into…well, digging deeper… here are some great resources:

Growing Out, Season 1: Growing in Jesus by Carl Simmons (Group)

The Cross Centered Life: Keeping the Gospel the Main Thing by C.J. Mahaney (Multnomah)

Sacred Pathways: Discover Your Soul's Path to God by Gary L. Thomas (Zondervan)

The Good and Beautiful God: Falling in Love With the God Jesus Knows by James Bryan Smith (InterVarsity)

Spiritual Discipleship by J. Oswald Sanders (Moody)

Multiplying God's Investment

The master was full of praise. 'Well done, my good and faithful servant. You have been faithful in handling this small amount, so now I will give you many more responsibilities. Let's celebrate together!' " (MATTHEW 25:21).

In this session, we'll journey...

from → **to**

recognizing the importance of growing out even further in our faith, our lives, and our impact...

exploring where God wants us to go next to use what he's given us.

Before gathering, make sure you have...

○ 1 penny for each person*

Optional activities (choose one or both):

○ **Option A:** white board or blackboard* (see page 144)

○ **Option B:** DVD of *Pay It Forward* (see page 154)

*See **Leader Notes**, page 174, for details.

Come and See

(about 15 minutes)

If you've chosen **Option A**, *read on.*
If you're doing **Option B**, *go to page 154.*

Be sure your white board or blackboard is already set up. If it's not, go to the **Leader Notes** on page 174 *now*.

›› Welcome back! Let's do a little math lesson.

You have two choices today. I can give you $1 billion, or I can give you one penny, triple it, and add it to the money you already have every year for the next 20 years. Which would you rather have: the $1 billion or the penny? (Pause for answers.)

Well, all I have are the pennies, so that's what you'll be getting today. I hope you're not too disappointed.

Give everyone a penny.

I'm pretty sure you'll be less disappointed when you see what could happen to that penny over the next 20 years.

Work through the math with your group on your white board or blackboard.

›› *Now* which would you rather have?

Pause for reactions, and then continue your discussion.

If there's any room left on your white board or blackboard, write people's answers, thanking them for their responses.

◎ What did it take for that growth to happen? Throw out some answers.

Come and See continued

Continue your discussion: ⟶

» **Think about it. If you poured your life in Jesus into just three people each year and each of them did the same thing...you can see the possibilities. And sure, some of the people you invest in won't give you a return on investment, but others will do even more than you anticipate as God leads them. So let's stay focused on the possibilities and dream a little today.**

We're going to start bringing it home this week. We've spent a season exploring how to bring others forward in Jesus. And if we've been taking these sessions to heart and applying them, we've already found ourselves in deeper, more meaningful relationships. It's also likely that God has stirred up something else within us—a desire to reach even more people with the love of Jesus. And that means expanding our circles of influence, maybe even taking leadership roles—because if God has put something on our hearts, he wants us to *do* something about it.

As you step into the mission God has called you to, you may be surprised to discover that God has been calling someone else—someone who was waiting for you to step out and step up. If we're willing to make that investment in others and help them see how they can impact others in the way God has called them to, there's no telling how big an impact our little contribution could make. And even if you never see it, that's OK. God sees it. And so does every person your life has touched, either directly or indirectly.

So for these last two sessions, let's explore where God might be leading each of us to invest our "pennies" next.

◎ How could we apply this idea to the *people* we invest in?

Seek and Find

(about 30 minutes)

> *[Jesus] matters because of what he brought and what he still brings to ordinary human beings, living their ordinary lives and coping daily with their surroundings. He promises wholeness for their lives.*
>
> *—Dallas Willard,* The Divine Conspiracy

» **Let's look at two passages—one at the very beginning of Jesus' earthly ministry and one near the end—both ultimately speaking to all of us. Can I have a couple of volunteers to read Luke 4:14-21 and then Matthew 25:34-40?** →

Get into your groups. (Pause.)

You might know people who are poor, imprisoned, blind, or oppressed, and you might feel a burden to reach out to them. Maybe you don't know these kinds of people personally, but you still feel a burden. Or maybe the people you're thinking about aren't actually suffering in those ways, but it's obvious that they're *spiritually* poor, imprisoned, blind, or oppressed. And they need Jesus just as much, if not more, right now.

 **Luke 4:14-21; Matthew 25:34-40**

◎ What connections do you see between Jesus' mission and ours? What differences do you see?

◎ Why do you think Jesus puts so much value on the people we tend not to value?

Seek and Find continued

In your groups, take 15 minutes to discuss these questions together: →

After 15 minutes, regain everyone's attention, keeping them in their groups. Ask for volunteers to share highlights and insights from their discussion time.

» **Before we go on, let's make this clear: You need to discover the answers God wants you to have. Not the *right* answer. Not the answer that will make you feel less guilty. Not even the answer to What should I do? But the answer to this: What has God put on your heart, and what does God want you to do about it? And, if that answer's not clear, you need to develop the ability to wait on God and enjoy his presence while you wait.**

Also begin thinking about the answers to these questions: Who can come alongside and help you? Who are the people in your life who can help in a hands-on way, help you think things through, encourage you, or tell you how they walked through it? Or who can become those people in your life, just like you've learned to become that person for someone else this season?

Let's take all this to heart and move forward, together.

"The church is a place of rehabilitation, not convalescence. It is not a hospice that prepares people to die; it is a rehab center preparing people to live."

—Rick Rusaw and Eric Swanson, The Externally Focused Church

◎ According to *your* definition, who are the poor, imprisoned, blind, or oppressed in your life?

◎ How have you seen *yourself* as poor, imprisoned, blind, or oppressed (or still do)?

◎ How has God been preparing you—investing in you, we might say again—to "proclaim… the Lord's favor" to others?

Go

(about 20 minutes)

[T]he important thing is not to think much, but to love much; do, then, whatever arouses you to love.

—Teresa of Ávila

» Staying in your groups, you're going to read again from Matthew 25—this time from verses 14-29.

After you read, discuss the questions that follow. After your discussion time, instead of selecting from the regular Walk It Out options, pray about what you just shared. How is God leading you to grow out even further? We'll talk more about this next session as well, but for now, use your time together to really pray about what God is doing in you and how he wants to use that to bring his grace to others. Use the penny you're still holding to remind you of what God is capable of doing with what he's given you, and take your pennies home this week as a reminder to keep praying about what God might want to do.

Take as much time as you need to pray together. When you're done, you're free to quietly leave [or quietly hang out until everyone's finished, if you're in a small-group setting]. →

Remember, it is impossible to celebrate God's work of transformation without confessing your need for more. No one is more ready to communicate God's grace than someone who has faced his own desperate need for it.

—Paul David Tripp, Instruments in the Redeemer's Hands

Matthew 25:14-29

◎ How have you already seen the "small amount" that God has trusted you with transform into something bigger?

◎ Why should we welcome "many more responsibilities" as God gives them to us?

◎ In what ways do you still take what God has given you and "[dig] a hole in the ground" to hide it?

◎ How might God want you to "dig out" and invest, so you can "celebrate together"? What will that investment cost you?

Because growing out means going out, I'll "Walk It Out" by:

____

____

____

____

____

SEEING IT DIFFERENTLY

Come and See–Option B

LEADER Instead of the penny activity in "Come and See," watch a scene from the movie *Pay It Forward.* (You'll still need your pennies, though.) Cue the movie to 30:00 (DVD Chapter 9), as Arlene comes out with the gun and yells, "Hey!" Stop the clip at 34:20, after Trevor shrugs and says, "So?"

GROUP

◎ Which of the reactions to Trevor's idea is closest to yours? Why?

Give everyone a penny.

GROUP

◎ How could we apply the idea of "paying it forward" to the people *we* invest in?

Pick up at the leader statement on page 146, beginning, **Think about it.**

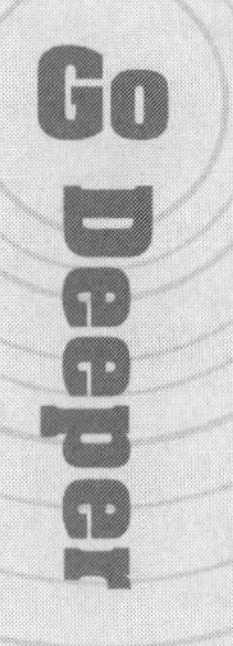

To dig deeper into how to "expand your investment portfolio," here are some great resources:

Outflow: Outward-Focused Living in a Self-Focused World by Steve Sjogren and Dave Ping (Group)

The Irresistible Revolution: Living as an Ordinary Radical by Shane Claiborne (Zondervan)

Simple Spirituality: Learning to See God in a Broken World by Christopher Heuertz (InterVarsity)

Hope Lives: A Journey of Restoration by Amber Van Schooneveld (Group)

Transforming Discipleship: Making Disciples a Few at a Time by Greg Ogden (InterVarsity)

The Never-Ending Story

"Jesus came and told his disciples, 'I have been given all authority in heaven and on earth. Therefore, go and make disciples of all the nations, baptizing them in the name of the Father and the Son and the Holy Spirit. Teach these new disciples to obey all the commands I have given you. And be sure of this: I am with you always, even to the end of the age' " (MATTHEW 28:18-20).

In this session, we'll journey...

from → **to**

reflecting on where God has taken us during this season...

exploring what's next (because there's *always* a next...).

Before gathering, make sure you have...

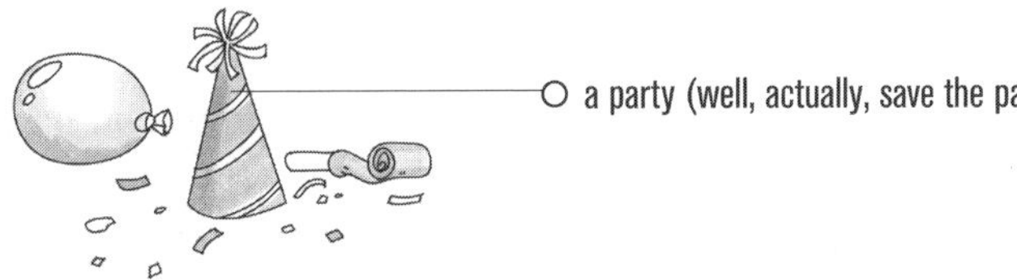

○ a party (well, actually, save the party for *after*)*

*See **Leader Notes**, page 176, for details.

Come and See

(about 15 minutes)

> *Seeing our lives as stories, rather than as an unrelated series of random events, increases the possibility for having in our lives what we find in the best stories: significant, purposeful action. We all want very much for it to have mattered that we were here.*
>
> —*Daniel Taylor,* The Healing Power of Stories

Have people set out the party foods they brought before you get started.

» **Congratulations! You've made it through this season! And there *will* be a party at the end of this session. But first, let's talk.**

Let's begin wrapping up the story of this season by talking about some other very important stories. Get into your groups, and discuss the following: →

Bring people back together after 10 minutes. Share highlights and insights from your discussion time.

» **It's been said that we might be the only Bible some people will ever read. That can be a scary thought, especially given some of the chapters that have already been written! But the good news is God is still writing our stories. We don't always understand why God adds or allows certain chapters in our lives, but we do know that he is crafting our stories so that they end well.**

And as with any good story, God builds on what he has already done. If we cooperate, our stories will always be moving forward, no matter how much activity other people might see or not see. So as we end this season together, we're excited to see what that next chapter in our lives might look like. Let's get ready to turn the pages together.

> *Every person we encounter is someone who is also on the verge of encountering Christ incognito.*
>
> —*Robert Gelinas,* Finding the Groove: Composing a Jazz-Shaped Faith

◎ What's your favorite story, and how does it end?

◎ How have you recently seen God working in your life, your relationships, even in your fellow group members? How has seeing that helped you grow?

◎ How does what God has been doing in you lately fit into the bigger story of your lifelong—your *eternal*—journey with Jesus?

Seek and Find

(about 15 minutes)

Ask for volunteers to read 2 Corinthians 3:8-18; 2 Corinthians 4:13-18; and Philippians 3:8-14. Then discuss ⟶

> *"You were made and set here for this, to give voice to your own amazement."*
>
> *—Annie Dillard,* The Writing Life

 **2 Corinthians 3:8-18, 4:13-18; Philippians 3:8-14**

◎ Where have you seen God's grace "reach more and more people" (2 Corinthians 4:15)?

◎ How does fixing your gaze on what God is going to do help you keep going right now?

◎ How does it also help you let go of your own expectations or fears and just smile and say, "OK God, whatever's next—bring it on"?

Go

(about 15+ minutes)

We do not want to be beginners. But let us be convinced of the fact that we will never be anything else but beginners, all our life!

—Thomas Merton, Contemplative Prayer

» **Once more, congratulations—during the course of this study, you've not only learned how to become stronger disciples of Jesus, but by walking through this together, sharing your lives in Jesus, and pushing each other forward, you've been equipped to become a better discipler of others. And with that, there's no better way to end this season than with Matthew 28:18-20. Who'd like to read it?**

Have your volunteer read Matthew 28:18-20.

» **Jesus is in control. Jesus is always with us, and he has given us a command. Therefore, we know how we need to walk from here. The only question left is, Where next? So get into your groups one last time, and take 10 minutes to discuss the following questions. And then we'll celebrate together!**

After 10 minutes, come back together as a large group. Before you start your party time, pray something such as:

prayer

» **Lord, we thank you that no matter what we do or where we go, you are with us always. We thank you also for those people you've put in our lives—whose examples, whose challenges, whose friendships help us keep growing further out—and closer to you. We thank you for the parts of our story you have yet to write, and we thank you for this opportunity to celebrate the parts you have already written.**

Be especially present with us as we enjoy our food and time together and as we celebrate the love you have for us and our love for one another. Help us to take that love wherever you send us next. In Jesus' name. Amen.

Now *party*!

Matthew 28:18-20

◎ What are you doing (or do you need to be doing) right now that you know Jesus wants you doing? Sum it up in a sentence or two; be specific.

◎ What do you think the next chapters in your story might look like? Who are the main players? Feel free to dream aloud here.

◎ How can we, as a group, continue to support and encourage each other?

Because God has not finished writing my story, I'll "Walk It Out" by:

____

____

____

____

____

____

Go Deeper

To dig deeper into understanding how your story fits into God's bigger story, here are some great resources:

To Be Told: God Invites You to Coauthor Your Future by Dan B. Allender (WaterBrook)

Epic: The Story God Is Telling by John Eldridge (Thomas Nelson)

Experiencing God: Knowing and Doing the Will of God by Henry Blackaby, Richard Blackaby, and Claude King (B&H Books)

Instruments in the Redeemer's Hands: People in Need of Change Helping People in Need of Change by Paul David Tripp (P&R Publishing)

General Tips

- **Read ahead.** Although these sessions are designed to require minimum preparation, read each one ahead of time. Highlight the questions you feel are especially important for your group to spend time on.
- **Preview DVD clips.** The copyright doctrine of fair use permits certain uses of very brief excerpts from copyrighted materials for not-for-profit teaching purposes without permission. If you have specific questions about your intended use of copyrighted materials, consult your church's legal counsel. Your church can obtain a blanket licensing agreement from Christian Video Licensing International for an annual fee. Visit cvli.com, or call 888-771-2854 for information.
- **Enlist others.** Don't be afraid to ask for volunteers. Who knows? They may want to commit to a role such as teaching a session or bringing snacks once they've tried it. However, give people the option to say, "No, thanks" as well.
- **Be prompt.** Always start on time. If you do this from the beginning, you'll avoid the tendency of group members to arrive later and later as the season goes on.
- **Gather supplies.** Make sure to have the supplies for each session on hand. (All supplies are listed on the opening page of each session.) Feel free to ask other people to help furnish supplies. This will give them even more ownership of the session.
- **Discuss child care.** If you're leading a small group, discuss how to handle child care—not only because it can be a sensitive subject but also because discussing options will give your group an opportunity to work together *as* a group.
- **Pray anytime.** Be ready and willing to pray at times other than the closing time. Start each session with

prayer—let everyone know they're getting "down to business." Be open to other times when prayer is appropriate, such as when someone answers a question and ends up expressing pain or grief over a situation he or she's currently struggling with. Don't save it for the end—stop and pray right there and then.

- **Let others talk.** Try not to have the first or last word on every question (or even most of them). Give everyone an opportunity to participate. At the same time, don't put anyone on the spot—remind people that they can pass on any questions they're not comfortable answering.
- **Stay on track.** There are suggested time limits for each section. Encourage good discussion, but don't be afraid to "rope 'em back in."
- **Hold people accountable.** Don't let your group off the hook with the assignments in the Walk It Out section—this is when group members apply in a personal way what they've learned. Encourage group members to follow through on their assignments.
- **Encourage group challenges.** Also note that "Do It Together"—the last weekly challenge in Walk It Out—is meant to be done as a group. Make sure that group members who take on these challenges are both encouraged and organized.
- **Pray.** Finally, research has shown that the single most important thing a leader can do for a group is to spend time in prayer for group members. So why not take a minute and pray for your group right now?

Session 1

- Read the General Tips starting on page 165, if you haven't already.
- If this is the first time you're meeting as a group, take a few minutes before your session to agree on a few simple ground rules. Here are three important ones:
  1. Don't say anything that will embarrass anyone or violate someone's trust.
  2. Likewise, anything shared in the group *stays* in the group, unless the person sharing it says otherwise.
  3. No one has to answer a question he or she is uncomfortable answering.
- At the beginning of this session, you're going to put people in the groups they'll be with for the rest of the season. They don't know this yet, but now *you* do. So think about how you might gently guide people into discipling relationships here. If your group has people of various ages, take advantage of it. Put older people with younger ones or more mature Christians with less mature ones. By doing so, you'll create spiritual friendships that could last well beyond this season. The reason we want to keep gender-specific groups is to help everyone feel free to share honestly and feel as safe as possible.
- For your activity in Go, you might put your pitcher of water in the middle of your group and leave them guessing for most of the session, or bring it out later—your call. Whenever you drop your tea bags in, don't give an explanation; just continue with the session. If you like, jostle your pitcher a bit while you're talking. During our field test, I dropped the tea bag in early on, during the white board discussion time in Seek and Find. It made a nice cup of tea for everyone by the time our session was finished.

  If people need prompting to answer the question, "What things had to take place for our tea bags to change the water?" here are a few ideas to get things started: You had to drop them in; they had to become saturated by the water; they had to spend some time in the water first. Our group got it quickly.

- On the other hand, the reactions from our group to the question in Seek and Find, ("Who do you know who seems ready to take the next step spiritually...?") were rather surprising, given this season's purpose. Specifically, most people *didn't have an answer.* That's OK—press on with the questions that follow. Get people thinking about what they can do to come along and invest in another person's spiritual growth an if they're not already doing it, *why aren't they*?

  I can't emphasize the importance of this session—and this season—enough. The lack of meaningful discipleship in the church today is *the* reason this entire curriculum was written. In fact, go back and read the intro "Why R.E.A.L. Discipleship Works" right now. This is what it's all about. And this season is graduation time—so let's get out there and *do it*!

Session 2

- If new people join the group this session, use part of the Come and See time to ask them to introduce themselves to the group. Have people pass their books around to record contact information (page 18). Give a brief summary of the points covered in Session 1.
- If you have newcomers this week, try to create new groups with them, if possible. If you only have one new man or woman, add him or her to one of your twosomes. On the other hand, if only one person from last week's group shows up, let him or her join another group this week.

  And while you may not need to worry about it this week, start thinking about this: If all of your groups have three people and someone new arrives, ask an existing group to volunteer to get into two sets of twos. The idea is not to rearrange groups but to *birth* them. This is a principle that will serve your group, and your church, well in the future.

Of course, if you're not sure if your visitor is going to stick around, it's OK to let a group be a foursome for a week or two before birthing a new one.

- On that note, we'd encourage you once more to take advantage of the Walk It Out section. Make it a take-home piece if you have to so you have enough group time elsewhere. Also, while we suggest doing this in pairs, you can approach it any way you like. This particular week in field-testing, we did it as an entire group and got a variety of interesting responses—as well as a heightened sense of accountability (now *everyone* knows what we committed to!).

Session 3

- I built in some extra time for the first question in Go on purpose. It will take a little time for people to think this through and express what they've got going on right now. But as they do, they'll likely bring up issues that they need to overcome to move forward—and which, in turn, will help the people they invest in. And sure enough, during our field-testing, we got a variety of answers to what group members would ask Paul, such as How can I forgive myself for what I've done the way God did and the way you've clearly forgiven yourself, too? And, How can I know God's mercy the way you do? One woman said she just wanted to follow Paul around and see his faith in action so she would know how to share her faith more openly. Your group members will come up with their own answers. Welcome them.
- Are you praying for your group members regularly? It's the most important thing a leader can do for his or her group. Take some time now to pray for your group, if you haven't already.

Session 4

- Now that you're a month into this season, you may find it helpful to make some notes right after your session to help you evaluate how things are going. Ask yourself, Did everyone participate? and Is there anyone I need to make a special effort to follow up with before the next session?

- This would also be a good opportunity to remind you that if you need to spend more time on a given session than just one week—and if you're not tied to a calendar and can spend some extra time—then *do it*! Taking the time to understand what God wants to tell your class, group, or accountability partner(s) is *way* more important than "covering the material."

- If it's an option, consider doing at least the first part of your session outside. You'll have more room for your paper airplane activity, and studies prove that natural sunlight actually helps the learning process. Besides, thinking back to your school days again, wasn't it fun to have class outside?

  On that note, our field test group had a lot of fun with the paper airplane activity. And it turns out that I'm an expert paper airplane engineer. Next time you're in Loveland, Colorado, come look me up, and I'll teach *you*, too.

- For your musical selection, find something expressive—a piece where listeners will be able to identify emotions and maybe even thoughts the composer or group experienced as they created the piece. Make sure there are *no* lyrics. Our field test group used Phil Keaggy's *Beyond Nature* album, which led to sharing about how the gentle, deliberate music reminded them of nature—and of the God who is, in C.S. Lewis' words, "beyond nature."

- Perhaps this isn't the type of admission one should make, but our group had no problems coming up with answers to the Go question, "Describe a time in your life when you definitely weren't imitating God—a time you wish you could get a do-over for." Tales of baby-Christian over-zealousness, clever acts of vengeance, and even instances where actions seemed OK but attitudes were terrible, abounded. That said, it set up some great discussion for the rest of this session. God has given us a lot to share with others. Even if it doesn't make us look good, it makes God look good. And the point *is* to glorify God, right?

Session 5

- Remember the importance of starting and ending on time, and remind your group of it, too, if you need to.
- If you normally open your time together in prayer (and if not, why not?), use the activity in Come and See for your opening prayer time instead.
- We had a few very quiet people in our field test group, and the activity in Seek and Find—where they *knew* they were being listened to—was the one when they really started to open up and share their thoughts and feelings with the others in the group. Coincidence?
- For your closing prayer time, consider asking for volunteers to pray for requests that were shared. You could also minimize the time you spend sharing prayer requests by just diving into prayer. Don't tell each other about the requests, just tell God, and let others listen. If certain requests need to be explained later on, spend some time afterward discussing those requests so people know how to pray for one another during the week.

Session 6

- For your opening activity, make sure your maps have a lot of streets; you want this activity to be a *little* challenging. A map with lots of parallel or cross streets would be ideal. You could get town maps from your local chamber of commerce, or photocopy a town map from your local phone book. We suggest cutting your map into about 25 pieces—enough to present a challenge, but not so difficult that groups can't figure it out. You may want to put your cut-up maps into resealable bags to keep the pieces together. Make sure there's enough table or floor space for groups to assemble their maps.
- This would be a good time to remind group members of the importance of following through on the weekly challenge each of them has committed to in Walk It Out.

Session 7

- Congratulations! You're halfway through this study. It's time for a checkup: How's the group going? What's worked well so far? What might you consider changing as you approach the remaining sessions?
- About your opening activity: Depending on how rhythmically talented you and your group are, you could mix it up more than this. For example, clap multiple times between the larger group's clapping. Don't be surprised if there are people in your group who simply can't keep a beat. Laugh with them, not at them—especially as they'll help make the point of your activity that much stronger. And if *you're* the person who can't keep a beat, ask a volunteer to help you lead. Again, it's OK to admit you're rhythmically challenged—your own openness will lead to more openness as you dig deeper into this session.
- For your activity in Seek and Find, if you have a small group, have all individuals in the other group(s) come up with solutions. If you have a group of more than 12, go ahead and use more than one "problem" group.

  Ideally you want one solution for each problem, but if the math isn't there just make sure every "problem" person has at least one "solution" group. Either way, the results will be humorous and yet will set up some serious discussion afterward.

Session 8

- If people need help getting started during your white board session in Seek and Find, throw out ideas such as encouragement, God's revelation, or loving confrontation.

  And after asking, "Why do you think there's such a variety here?" don't settle for "Because people are different." Drill down deeper. Get specific. *Why* is it better to confront, encourage, or step back and let God work in a given situation?

Session 9

- Thanks for your obedience in reading these instructions. Now here they are: ***Don't follow through with the trust fall in Come and See.*** Just say something like, "Good news, everyone—you're not going to need to do the trust fall." Then ask everyone to sit back down, and continue your discussion. Say something like, "Sorry to get you all concerned; it was the only way to keep the suspense. The good news is that the suspense will fuel the discussion you're about to have. So go ahead and enjoy your discussion time together."
- Take all the time you need to work through this session. People may not be facing this issue now, but they almost certainly will at some point. And there's a very good chance that some people in your group are facing something like this right now. They need wisdom. They need to understand their own limitations. Very possibly, they need to deal with the guilt they feel about letting another person down, even if they've done everything possible. And they need your support, both as individuals and as a group. Take the time to give it to them.
- Speaking of support, how are you doing with your prayer time for the group? Take some time to pray for your group now, if you haven't done so already.
- One more thing: At some point this season, you've probably noticed the section at the end called Go Deeper. Today I'm going to be pushy about it. If you're truly serious about helping those facing crisis, inside or outside your group, pick up at least one of the selections in *Group's Emergency Response Handbook* series. There are books for all circumstances, from small groups to children's ministry to disaster relief, containing first-hand accounts, counseling tips, as well as advice on what to say, what not to say, and when to refer. I can't recommend them to you highly enough, and not just because they're Group books. I wish I'd had these *before* I came to Group.

Session 10

- For extra impact, pick one or more of your representatives to lead today's session. You could have one person lead the entire session or have a different person lead each section, depending on the size of your group. Model what you're teaching today. Let go of the reins a bit.

Session 11

- For your opening "snack-tivity," provide a wide variety of toppings with your ice cream, such as cherries, hot fudge, nuts, sprinkles, and marshmallows. Also make sure there are different kinds of toppings, not just different kinds of sweet stuff. If it's too early in the day for ice cream (although really, is it *ever*?), try an alternative that would lend itself to different kinds of toppings, such as yogurt or pancakes. If cost is an issue, share the wealth; ask each group member to bring a different topping.
- Now is a good time to do another group checkup—especially if you're planning on doing another season together after this one. Ask yourself (and the group, if it makes sense to do so—but phrase it differently if you do), Is everyone participating? and, Is there anyone I need to make a special effort to follow up with?

Session 12

- Since your next session will be your group's last one in this book, you'll probably want to start discussing with the group what to do after you've completed this study. Will you go on to Season 5? "pull over" and study another subject in more depth? break up and head to different classes? Make your plans now.
- Note that participants will be keeping the pennies you give them during Come and See, so make sure you have enough and know you're not getting them back. If your group is big enough, you'll also want to have a container to pass around your pennies.

- Before the session, write the numbers 1 through 20 vertically along the left side of your board. Leave room for two columns. Across from "Year 1" write ".01" in your first column and "$1,000,000,000" in the second column. To make it easy for you, here are the actual numbers for the first column:

Year 1 = .01	Year 11 = $10,485.76
Year 2 = .04	Year 12 = $41,943.04
Year 3 = .16	Year 13 = $167,772.16
Year 4 = .64	Year 14 = $671,088.64
Year 5 = $2.56	Year 15 = $2,684,354.56
Year 6 = $10.24	Year 16 = $10,737,418.24
Year 7 = $40.96	Year 17 = $42,949,672.96
Year 8 = $163.84	Year 18 = $171,798,691.84
Year 9 = $655.36	Year 19 = $687,194,767.36
Year 10 = $2,621.44	Year 20 = $2,748,779,069.44

  For the second column, you can just write "$1,000,000,000" for Year 20, and then draw an arrow. Unless, of course, you *want* to write "$1,000,000,000" 20 times.

  Don't show all these numbers to the group before your session. You can write them all beforehand if you like, but keep years 2 through 19 of your "penny" column covered until after you've given everyone a penny.

  If group members can't think of an answer to "What did it take for that growth to happen?" other than "time," here are some other answers to prompt them: patience, faith, persistence. You want them thinking this question through to set up the question that follows.

- Take an advance look at the Leader Notes for Session 13. You'll probably want to do some advance planning for your group's party.

Session 13

- Since this is your group's last session in this book, make sure you have a plan for next week...and beyond.
- Let's talk about that party. Usually at the end of each season, we suggest that you do something special after your meeting time, or at another time. This time, though, we're *demanding* that you party. You're finishing Season 4 of *Growing Out*—meaning, even if you don't go on to the "graduate levels" of Seasons 5 (Leadership) and 6 (Mission), you've graduated *From Disciples to Disciplers.* We don't want to play up the graduating thing too much—because again, you'll *always* be growing, *always* be a beginner in some way—but you *have* crossed a major milestone here, and that's a major cause for celebration.

  Therefore, we've built in some extra time at the end of this session for your celebration. Even if it's only a 15-minute party, *do it.* Try to plan an extended time together, though. Start your time earlier or end later if you have to. But you are *commanded* to party!

  Also make a point of getting everyone involved. Let people bring whatever's appropriate to your final session—snacks, drinks, breakfast food, even serious munchie food like hot wings or barbecue. And feel free to decorate your meeting area, too—make it festive. Give out party favors, if you're really ambitious. Whatever you do, create the same sense of anticipation this entire session is built around. Celebrate what God has done—and what he's going to do next! And may each of you experience God's blessings as he does it!